2/5

18400

THE FUNERAL

THE WESTMINSTER SOURCE BOOKS

THE FUNERAL, by Andrew W. Blackwood
THE CHRISTIAN SACRAMENTS, by Hugh Thomson Kerr
PASTORAL WORK, by Andrew W. Blackwood
THE PUBLIC WORSHIP OF GOD, by Henry Sloane Coffin
THE CRAFT OF SERMON ILLUSTRATION,
by W. E. Sangster
THE CRAFT OF SERMON CONSTRUCTION,
by W. E. Sangster

(Other volumes in preparation)

The Funeral

A Source Book for Ministers

ANDREW WATTERSON BLACKWOOD

Chairman of the Practical Department
The Theological Seminary, Princeton, New Jersey
Professor of Biblical Homiletics
Temple University School of Theology
Philadelphia, Pennsylvania

The Westminster Press · Philadelphia

*Dedicated
to my students
past and present*

Acknowledgments

THE writer is indebted to the following for permission to quote. If he has neglected to secure permission from any other, he will rectify the error when it is called to his notice.

American Tract Society: Poems from *Bees in Amber*, by John Oxenham.

Barnes, A. S., and Co.: Two cuts from *Song and Service Book for Ship and Field,* ed. by Chaplain Ivan L. Bennett. 1941.

Coolidge, Mrs. Grace: A poem, "The Open Door."

Freeman, Mrs. Margery: Two poems by Robert Freeman.

Houghton Mifflin Co.: "The Butterfly," from *A Marriage Cycle*, by Alice F. Palmer; "Resignation," by H. W. Longfellow; two poems by J. G. Whittier.

Little, Brown and Co.: "Going to Heaven," from *Poems by* Emily Dickinson.

Macmillan Company, The: Excerpt from *The Art of Ministering to the Sick*, by R. C. Cabot and R. L. Dicks; four poems by C. Rossetti; two poems by Alfred Tennyson; "At a Burial," from *Poems* by William Watson.

Methodist Publishing Company: Two prayers from *The Ritual*.

Osborn, H. F.: A poem by his brother, Will C. Osborn.

Scribners: "Emancipation," from *Thoughts for Every-day Living*, by M. D. Babcock; a selection from *Poems* by Sidney Lanier; two selections from *The Poems of Henry van Dyke*.

The author is grateful for implied permission to quote from many sources, notably prayers, not under copyright. Other obligations appear in the text. The chief is to the one who suggested the writing and helped with the plans.

Contents

Foreword

THE request for this book has come from the publishers. They report that many pastors desire a comprehensive treatment of the funeral and related matters. Especially do young ministers wish such a guidebook. Out in the laboratory of life they are learning by trial and error what they should have known in part before they were ordained. "In every art there is a knack that is not a gift."

Fortunately, it is possible to master any practical subject during the first few years in the parish. That is what the majority of us have had to do. In my early pastoral experiences I should have welcomed a book showing how mature clergymen solve problems relating to the funeral. Strange as it may seem to lovers of theory, the most perplexing questions that come to the parish ministers have to do with the old word "How?"

Many pastors feel that the teaching of practical theology has been too theoretical. Some of the ablest lecturers and writers in the field steer away from things practical. They speak of the "how-to" books as superficial, and keep writing about other things. Surely someone ought to prepare ministerial treatises as scholarly and readable as are at hand in the field of medicine. In that profession things practical enjoy prestige.

In medicine no names are more revered than those of Cabot and Osler, each of whom has written about practical methods of healing. In our field the problems are more elusive, but still we can learn from the masters of medical literature. We too should prepare the student to deal with the person who is in need; we should stress the normal rather than the abnormal; we should make large use of typical cases; and we should provide clinical training under expert supervision.

"What can be learned can be taught." In years to come the minister will be trained for his practical duties as thoroughly as his brother who studies medicine or surgery. Meanwhile my sympathy goes out to young men of promise who have entered the greatest work in the world with little concern about the mundane matters that must occupy many of their waking hours. Nowhere does the lack of training seem more glaring than when a young minister stands face to face with death, and knows not what to do.

Such are the practical problems and ideals that have led to the writing of the book. The work of preparation has enlisted my heart. I have enjoyed recalling the days when I was a parish minister and becoming familiar with the work of masters now on the field. I believe that on the average the ministry today is stronger than at any time in recent years, and that the pastors of tomorrow will be still better trained. I hope that this book about the funeral will cheer and help many a man of God in his ministry of Christian comfort and hope.

ANDREW WATTERSON BLACKWOOD.

The Theological Seminary,
Princeton, New Jersey.

I. The Funeral Problem

AMONG all the problems of the parish minister few are more baffling than those that concern funerals. Not every occasion proves difficult, but in the course of the year any pastor is likely to face perplexing problems. This is especially true of the first few years. If a man learns as he goes along he will gradually become accustomed to meeting each situation as it arises. Meantime, the difficulties connected with funerals should help to make a man humble. They should also send him to his knees.

How can a minister hope to solve such problems? Before we turn to suggestions about ways and means, we ought to think further about the basic principles. Since we are approaching the matter from the viewpoint of the pastor, we shall start with him. But we should remember that the interests of the sorrowing friends are of vastly more concern. Most vital of all are the claims of God.

THE MINISTER

What is expected of the minister at a funeral? Instead of thinking abstractly, let us consider a case. When William James died, his widow sent a note to George A. Gordon, of the New Old South Church in Boston: "I want you to officiate at the funeral, as one of William's friends, and also as a man of faith. That is what he was. I want no hesitation or diluted utterance at William's funeral." What an ideal for any pastor: to be a friend, as well as a man of faith, with no hesitation or diluted utterance!

Conversely, when Robert Burns lay dying he spoke about his obsequies. Referring to a company of ill-trained vol-

unteer soldiers, he said: "Don't let that awkward squad fire
a salute over my grave." While the poet was not thinking
of any clergyman, every minister should take these words to
heart. Otherwise he and the others who share in the final
ceremonies may seem like members of an awkward squad.
From this point of view there are two kinds of ministers:
the one knows how to conduct a funeral; the other does not.

The difficulties are of many sorts. Some of them relate to
time. The call from the home of sorrow may come without
warning. For weeks the pastor may toil with little to break the
daily routine. Then there may be a succession of funerals.
Even though there is nothing unusual, every such experience
ought to move his heart. Sometimes he scarcely knows what
to do or say. If he had a week or two he might be able to
solve the new problem, but meanwhile he must act, once
for all.

These perplexing situations are not so common as the
present discussion makes them appear. But they do come.
Among the harrowing experiences which the writer has had
at funerals, the most perplexing were in his early ministry at
Pittsburgh. Within half a year, owing to the character of the
neighborhood surrounding the church, he officiated at the
obsequies of six persons who had come to death through
violence.

Each case was different. In none of the six was there anything especially reprehensible. Still the young pastor longed
for the wisdom of a Solomon and the heart of a shepherd. As
he grew older, the annual number of funerals increased, but
the proportion of perplexing situations became smaller. Like
the family physician, the minister who is faithful learns how
to heal the broken in heart. Even so, it should never seem
easy to make ready for a funeral, and thus to lead the sorrowing friends close to the heart of God.

The following experience was unique. A graduate of a
divinity school had never officiated at a funeral, and he knew
practically nothing about the subject. In August he went out

to his first charge. For two weeks he was the only clergyman in town. During the first ten days he had ten funerals. In each situation he found something different, and in most cases he was perplexed. To this day he doubtless feels that someone back in the seminary should have forewarned him about what he might soon have to face.

No small part of the problem may be due to the shortness of time for preparation. Before his first funeral the writer had only fifteen minutes. During that interval he felt that he should shave and dress as for a vital ceremony. He did not wish to seem less suitably attired than the mortician. Before the young parson was ready the carriage was waiting at the door. As for spiritual preparation, he had never learned to pray while shaving, but he did have a few minutes of quietness on the way to the home.

Like Abraham, the young minister went out by faith, not knowing whither. He claimed the promise: "It shall be given you in that same hour what ye shall speak." But on the way home he resolved that by God's grace he would never again go to a house of grief so totally unprepared. As for the way to get ready for unexpected funerals, that is shown throughout the present book. It represents what the writer wishes someone had taught him while in the seminary.

Even in the case of a normal funeral there may be only a little time for preparation. If a person falls asleep on Wednesday evening local custom may call for services on Thursday afternoon. This is all the time that usually elapses between death and burial in certain parts of the South. Meanwhile the pastor has other things to do. How can he get ready for what is to be a neighborhood event?

When there is an opportunity to prepare there may be a paucity of suitable materials. Even at the seminary library, with half a day at his disposal, a man who is familiar with the books in the practical department may not know where to lay his hands on what he wishes to use at a complex funeral. Much more likely is this to be the case early in a man's first

pastorate. For a year or so books may be few. There may not
be near at hand a friendly older minister to whom the young
man can telephone for advice. This is the pastor's zero hour.

If there are materials there may be no plan. The more facts
and ideas a man has in mind, the more he may become be-
wildered. Unless he has had experience in using such resources to meet human needs, he may not know how to prepare a simple program. If he is able, after a fashion, he may
not feel that he has time without neglecting his other duties.
Doubtless he will muddle through. But a death comes only
once; there should be no ministerial muddling. Our God is
not a muddler.

Is there in the ministry anything vital that receives as little
attention as making ready for many a funeral? In preparing
to preach, the clergyman mulls over his subject for days, if
not for weeks or months. In looking forward to the celebration of the Lord's Supper, he is even more zealous about
making ready in advance. He may not know that his prestige,
locally, depends largely on his ability to do and say the right
thing at every neighborhood funeral.

We are taking for granted that the pastor is a sincere
Christian, and that he has been called of God to be a minister.
Even so, at times he may have psychological handicaps. For
instance, he may be called into the home of strangers. There
he may feel unready to administer comfort. Then if ever he
needs to serve as a friend and a man of faith, without hesitation or diluted utterance. Instead of cherishing an inferiority
complex, he ought to cultivate a holy self-respect.

Whether in the study making ready or in the home conducting the service, no man is able to do his best work when
he is bothered, and feels conscious of his mental processes. At
a funeral people wish to know that the minister in charge is
master of the situation and of himself. It is so with the engineer in a railway locomotive. In the recent autobiography of
Irvin S. Cobb, *Exit Laughing,* he says that of all the crafts-
men in America the locomotive engineer makes the strongest

impression of mastery. It is much the same with the captain of
an ocean liner. He knows. He is able. He is ready. Should it
not be so with the pastor in the presence of death?

The most experienced clergyman may receive a summons
that will cause him perplexity. He may know the books, and
he may have solved many problems in ways all his own. But
the present case is unique. Like the physician when he finds
conditions that differ from anything in the textbooks, the
minister feels that under God he must work out his own
salvation. There is no one stereotyped way of ministering to
friends or strangers in sorrow. There are no patent formulas.
Every funeral should be somewhat unique. Herein lies much
of the difficulty.

Without pausing now to consider possible solutions of
these problems, let us fix in mind two texts. Each of them has
to do with using available resources in meeting the heart
needs of men. The first text is from the spiritual autobiography of the Apostle Paul. The other passage is from the
most tender and moving of all his letters to Christian friends.

"My grace is sufficient for thee: for my strength is made
perfect in weakness" (II Cor. 12: 9a). Here is abundance of
divine power for all a minister's needs. The other text voices
a man's faith, which is human weakness laying hold on divine power to supply his needs: "I can do all things through
Christ which strengtheneth me" (Phil. 4: 13).

THE SORROWING FRIENDS

Still more serious may be the questions that concern the
friends who have just parted from their loved one. As a
matter of course they may be strangers, but in alluding to
them as friends one is holding up the ideal. After the funeral
they should be loyal supporters of the pastor and the local
church.

Whether strangers or not, they are likely to feel confused.
At times they seem to be beside themselves. For weeks or
months they have been wearing themselves out in attendance

on their loved one. In another kind of situation, still more difficult for the pastor to meet, the blow has fallen without warning. Yesterday the husband and father was hale and happy. He had never known what it meant to be weak and ill. In his office today just before noon he dropped dead. Is it any wonder that the widow cries out, "My God, my God, why?"

Even if the circumstances are not exceptional, still the bereaved may be confused. They may never have had a death in the home. They know nothing about morticians, burial plots, and funeral services. The widow may never have handled any money of her own. She may never have made an important decision without first consulting her husband. As she sits among the ashes of her hopes for the morrow she is in no condition to decide about what must be done today.

Some of the perplexities relate to money. In one case there is little or none. The long illness has eaten up the household savings. The person in charge does not know which way to turn. If the pastor is aware of the circumstances he may suggest to the deacons that they consider extending financial aid. The situation, however, is delicate. Even in the hour of sorrow self-respecting folk do not wish to think of themselves as on relief. Really they are members of the church household, and they should be ready to receive what they would gladly give if the facts were reversed. In any case, the minister himself should not become mixed up in matters relating to money.

In another home of sorrow there may be more money for disposal than ever before. If the husband has been frugal there may be various sorts of insurance funds. When these resources become available all at once, the inexperienced widow may lose her head. She may say to herself, "This is all I can do now for my dear husband." Around her may be a small host of relatives and neighbors who keep proffering advice. As each new group arrives there may be still more counsel that seems new and strange. If it is not followed in detail there may be ruffled feelings.

The most officious neighborhood advisers make it their business to visit any home in sorrow. This is more likely to be the case in a rural community, or in the residential district of a city, than among those who dwell in vast apartment buildings, where the feeling may be one of isolation. In either case, the attention of the persons who mourn may be fixed upon things of the earth.

In an occasional household there is only a semblance of grief. At heart the relatives are relieved. Although they strive to conceal their feelings, they find it hard not to look happy. Privately they say, "At last the old man is gone; now we can get his dough." Who but the pastor knows how an elderly man lingers on in a family circle where his room and his money would be more welcome than his presence? Perhaps the only real religion beneath the roof has been in the heart of the aged invalid.

Whatever the background, the funeral is likely to be an event in the community. The good name of the Lord Jesus, the prestige of the local church, and the influence of the pastor, all depend in part on the minister's ability to conduct a funeral. If he is wise he devotes a good deal of spare time to making ready for such a ministry. If he becomes a master of every funeral assembly, his influence for good will be widespread.

At many a service of farewell the throng is cosmopolitan. More than at any other time men and women come home from afar. They feel that the occasion is unique; to each friend death comes only once. Many of those present never attend church. Except for an occasional funeral service, they have no contact with religion. They are as sheep without a shepherd. If the minister is able to move their hearts God-ward, they will remember him as long as they live. But in less than thirty minutes it is far from easy for the pastor to supply the needs of all the waiting hearts.

THE MYSTERY

We have thought about the difficulties that concern the minister and the sorrowing friends. Still more serious are the problems that have to do with death itself. It is a mystery. Who can tell what is the meaning of death? It is the end of a man's life on earth, and the beginning of his eternal existence elsewhere. But what is life, here and hereafter? No one can tell. According to the Anglo-Saxons, a man's sojourn on earth is like the flight of a bird at night. Out of the darkness and the unknown the winged one comes into the banquet hall, circles for a while amid the shadows above the central fire, and then flies out again into the darkness and the unknown.

According to the Christian faith, a human soul comes from God at birth and goes back to God at death. This way of looking at the facts is religious. It stresses the other world. In recent years such an old-fashioned view of life may seem outmoded. Whatever the reason, many a man never thinks or speaks about death unless he must. In large measure he seems to have adopted the Christian Scientist's attitude towards the final mystery of earth: "There is no such thing as death." But still the fact and the mystery persist.

The spirit of our time is secular. For instance, compare the best sellers among present-day novels with the tales of Charles Dickens. Where among current fiction is there so much stress on deathbed scenes as in Dickens? He may have kept his readers too long at the deathbed of Little Nell. If so, the novelist was a man of his day.

The same contrast appears in the pulpit. Where among published sermons today can you find such emphasis on death as in the printed discourses of Spurgeon? For example, in his most famous message, "Songs in the Night," there are two deathbed scenes. In his preaching, as in his choice of hymns and in his public prayers, Spurgeon was a man of his time. He believed with William Sanday, the Oxford scholar, that in the New Testament the center of gravity is beyond the grave.

Doubtless Spurgeon and Dickens went too far. Nevertheless, neither was afraid to face the mystery of death. If the present-day minister would give the subject the prominence that it has in the New Testament, he would help to prepare each of the friends for the change that is sure to come erelong, either in his own case or in that of one who is dearer than all else on earth. When shall we Protestant ministers learn that the glory of the Christian faith lies veiled in mystery?

The mystery is not so much about death as what lies beyond. Perhaps this is why the Book refers to the experience in terms of motion and the forward look. Here are some of the Biblical figures for death: starting on a journey, crossing a river, going home, falling asleep, or being transformed from an earthly seed into a heavenly flower. Whatever the figure, wrapped up in it lies a fact. The fact concerns the life everlasting.

The word "mystery" points to a lofty Christian truth that no man is able to discover for himself, but that God makes known through his Holy Bible. Among all the mysteries of the Christian faith, some of the most precious cluster round the reality of heaven. From the human point of view these are the most glorious truths that the Lord Jesus came to reveal. At a funeral service the question is, how can the minister hope in so brief a time to make eternal verities clear and luminous in the eyes of men and women who may be thinking about things of time and space?

Even in the light of the Resurrection, and of the New Testament which makes it known, there are many questions that the minister cannot answer. Some of the most perplexing have to do with heaven. Is it a place? If so, where do its islands lift "their fronded palms in air"? If the body sleeps in the grave until the resurrection, how does the soul survive without a personal habitation? Will the children of God recognize each other in the Father's home? How can the

redeemed in glory be at peace if they know that loved ones
who tarry on in the flesh are not making ready to live forever with God?

The facile way to deal with such issues is to ignore them.
In any funeral there is sure to be something interesting on
the human level. At the services in memory of a businessman
the front part of the church was filled with flowers and the
rest of the sanctuary was thronged with neighbors and
friends. Downtown he had been highly esteemed and in the
church he had been active as a trustee. Without referring
directly to him, the minister spoke for ten or twelve minutes
on "The Religion of a Businessman."

The text was one of the supreme verses in the Old Testament: "What doth the Lord require of thee, but to do justly,
and to love mercy, and to walk humbly with thy God?"
(Micah 6: 8). The heart of the message was that a businessman's religion starts with justice. He determines to be right
with God, right with men, right with self. Such religion expresses itself in kindness, and reaches its culmination in humility. For the Christian the way to achieve such a standard
is through Christ and the Cross.

That evening the treasurer of the church, also a businessman, said to the minister, "If you can give me as good a
final send-off, my friends will feel that I have not lived in
vain." The pastor was pleased. But the next day when he
called at the home to which sorrow had come he changed his
mind about that funeral message. He decided that he had
dodged the real issue, and that he had missed the mark.

At the door the first member of the household to greet
him was the daughter, ten years of age. When she saw her
friend, the minister, she ran to greet him, and exclaimed,
"Where is my daddy today?" What did she care about the
religion of a businessman? For the first time in all her happy
days she had come face to face with the eternal mystery. She
wished to be sure that her father was safe in the keeping of
the Lord Jesus.

Fortunately, the evasive attitude toward death and the hereafter is not so common now as a few years ago. Many a pastor has rediscovered the value of the individual soul. In the songs of the sanctuary and in the prayers of the pastor there may be much about the forgiveness of sins, the resurrection of the body, and the life everlasting. In the pulpit work, also, from time to time there is luminous teaching about heaven as home. Throughout both prayers and preaching there is a spirit of mystery and wonder.

Thus we have thought about the funeral problem. It relates to the minister who officiates, to the people who mourn, and to the mystery that envelops death. In view of these facts it is not strange that the conduct of a single funeral takes out of the pastor untold energy. From such an experience he will emerge either a better man or a worse. His purpose in conducting the service is to glorify God and thus help the sorrowing friends. To his own heart also the experience should be a means of grace.

The funeral ceremony brings out whatever there is in a man of strength or of weakness. The content and the spirit of all that he does and says reveal the truth or unreality of his doctrinal beliefs, the warmth or coldness of his spiritual experience, the breadth or narrowness of his Biblical knowledge, the sincerity or sham of his sympathies, and his resourcefulness or lack of skill as a leader in worship.

Despite all the difficulties, or perhaps because of them, there is nothing that the retired clergyman misses more than the privilege of being among people who stand face to face with the last great enemy, and are sore afraid. Next to the satisfactions of being a parish minister, the veteran would welcome the opportunity to confer with any young pastor who is perplexed about funeral problems. Happy is a young minister if in his first charge there is near at hand such an older brother who is ready to sympathize and confer in any time of need.

The spirit of the retired clergyman may be that of Lyman

Abbott. When he wrote the following he was eighty years of age: "I enjoy my home, my friends, my life. I shall be sorry to part from them. But I have always stood in the bow looking forward with hopeful anticipation. When the time comes for me to put out to sea, I think I shall still be standing in the bow and looking forward with eager interest and glad hopefulness to the new world to which the unknown voyage will take me" (II Tim. 4: 7, 8).

Inspirational Readings

Brown, Charles R., *The Making of a Minister*. The Century Co., 1927. Chapter XI.
McAfee, Cleland B., *Ministerial Practices*. Harper & Brothers, 1928. Chapters XIX, XX.

II. The Christian Pastor

THE man who has the shepherd heart knows what to do at a deathbed or a funeral. The minister who is not helpful at such a time is probably not a diligent pastor. To these broad statements there is one exception. They do not refer to the man who has had little experience. During the first year or two in the active ministry the majority of us belonged to the awkward squad. Nowhere else did we seem so little at home as in the presence of death. But if a man trusts the Lord and loves people he can learn how to be helpful at a deathbed and in the funeral service.

Failure to be useful at such a time may be due to no lack of ability. In one of our largest cities an active lay officer is devoted to his minister, a brilliant preacher. But when the layman's wife was on her deathbed, he wished that he could invite a neighboring clergyman who excels in pastoral sympathy. After the funeral services, which were coldly intellectual, the layman went in private more than once to the home of the man with the shepherd heart. A real pastor approaches a deathbed or a funeral as a friend, not as a plenipotentiary.

For the neglect of the pastoral office some of us older ministers may be responsible. We have stressed other things. According to Charles R. Brown, of Yale, the favorite form of indoor amusement for clergymen a few years ago was to poke fun at the habit of ringing doorbells. In a city church the present custom is to have the people come to see the pastor. That is good. Somehow or other he should care for the sheep. Meanwhile no one has accepted Dean Brown's challenge: "Will someone be good enough to find me strong,

stable, growing, generous, spiritually-minded churches where
no pastoral calling has been done in the past ten years? I
do not know of any such."

Fortunately, the Protestant Church is witnessing a revival
of the pastoral ministry. Theologically, there has been a
rediscovery of the individual soul. At the same time there is
a feeling that the prospective pastor should be as well trained
for his duties as his brother who expects to become a physician. The man who ministers to the soul ought to enter the
home as a personal friend. In the presence of death there is
no room for mere professionalism.

What, then, are the traits that mark the helpful pastor?
At present we are thinking about him as he ministers in the
presence of death. We shall consider seven qualities, each
of which the minister can cultivate. We shall begin with the
most vital and come down to the most external.

SPIRITUALITY

To be an effective pastor a man needs to be filled with the
Holy Spirit. The reference is to no esoteric experience, and to
no extreme theory. The meaning is that he ought to have
had a personal experience of God's redeeming grace, and
that he should be renewing the experience from day to day.
Body and soul, he should belong to the Lord and the people
in the local church. Whenever there is a call to an upper
room where death is near, or to a home where it has come,
he should be ready to serve as the man of God.

Such a pastor is a living epistle. He is known and read
by everybody in the community. Day after day the minister
shows the meaning and glory of Christian manhood. Because
he lives in constant fellowship with Christ, the pastor's life
is radiant. By his daily ministry he shows what the Fourth
Gospel means when it says that for the child of God the life
everlasting has already begun. Such a radiant personality was
Phillips Brooks. In his presence it was not difficult to believe
in the reality and nearness of the spiritual world. At a death-

bed, in a funeral service, or anywhere else, such a pastor is a living benediction.

SYMPATHY

The man filled with the Spirit of God is a lover of people. He becomes increasingly like God, and God is Love. The man with the shepherd heart knows his sheep one by one. He is eager to share sorrows as well as joys. Especially does his heart go out to the friend who is dying, and to the loved ones after the end has come. Into the home of grief he comes as a personal friend, not as a professional stranger.

Such a man wins his way into the hearts of people while they are hale and active. When he first enters a field he resolves that by God's grace he will almost never be called into a home where he is a stranger. If he knows and loves the people, one by one, he will be able to help in any zero hour. If he prays with them in normal times he will know how to intercede at a deathbed, or a funeral service. If he has spoken on behalf of Christ to every unsaved person in the community, the minister will know what to say in the presence of death. At such a time it is the shepherd's heart that counts.

The helpful pastor is like his Saviour, a friend that sticketh closer than a brother. On the manward side, the chief fact about such a minister is sympathy. That means putting oneself in the other person's place, looking at his world through his eyes, feeling as he ought to feel, and doing all one can to bring him out into the sunlight of God's love. Sympathy is only another name for personal Christianity in action. That in turn is the meaning of the Golden Rule.

Pastoral sympathy calls for the use of imagination, or insight. How else can the unmarried minister, such as Phillips Brooks, comfort a young mother who has lost her little babe? How can a man, even though a husband and father, enter into the experience of a mother who knows there will never be another babe to fill the arms that are empty now? When the pastor's heart is overflowing with sympathy quickened daily at the Cross, he can enter into any "life situation." Better still, he can bring to the broken heart God's healing balm.

Even when the minister is called into a home where he is a stranger, he should know what to do and say. Through no fault of his own he is not as yet a personal friend. But he will be from this time forward. Just now he is present as one who longs to bring these persons close to the heart of God. Once again the secret of being a good pastor is sympathy. It was at the grave of Lazarus that the Lord Jesus wept. While the pastor may not weep, he should make clear how much he cares when any heart is broken.

Such a minister expresses sympathy by sending personal letters. Early in his lifework he learns to put into permanent form anything that his friends in sorrow may wish to preserve. Even though he may live near by he wishes them to have in their home a visible token that he has loved and revered the father who has gone home to God. In later years no minister has ever regretted the time and care devoted to the writing of pastoral letters.

A few years ago a schoolmaster died. In going through his papers the loved ones found a number of personal messages from the pastor. Whenever anything worthy of note had come into the life of the schoolman, or into his family circle, the minister had sent him a note of felicitation or sympathy. Perhaps because that was the pastor's custom with all his friends, he did not remember those letters. But when the husband and father was no longer with them in the flesh, the other members of the household cherished those visible signs of the place he had occupied in the heart of the minister.

In short, when a pastor trusts the Lord and loves the people, one by one, he knows what to do and say at a deathbed or in a funeral service. He feels that he is among friends. When there is an opportunity to make ready, he does so as well as he can. He wishes to represent the Lord worthily.

Beneath all his intellectual preparation is the willingness to let the heart have its way. Would that there were in every parish a minister excelling in the fine art of Christian sympathy!

INTELLIGENCE

The effective pastor needs also a high degree of intelligence. The surest proof of mental acumen is the ability to solve each problem as it arises. The reference here is only to the funeral and related matters. If a man is able to do and say the right thing in one service after another, he evidently possesses a high degree of intelligence. If he had time for extended research among books, and for conference with brethren of piety and experience, it might be possible to employ collective wisdom. But as a rule the minister must rely on himself, as the servant of God. When the time comes for him to act, he must be ready.

Many of the problems that test a man's intellectual powers will appear in later chapters. If he were content to treat every situation according to a set of principles worked out by somebody else, he would be like a physician who has only one way of treating all sorts of diseases. But if the physician of souls is to be an expert in sizing up each new situation, and in using holy words to heal human hearts, he must know how to think, and that with precision.

From a different point of view, the minister needs to have a sound philosophy of life. If he is to serve as the local interpreter of the Christian faith, especially as it relates to death and the hereafter, he must know what the Scriptures teach about time and eternity, and what reason there is for the hope of life everlasting with God. In the presence of the last great enemy, if the minister is not to seem like a blind leader of the blind, he must know the truth that makes men free. He must have brain power, and use it all for the glory of God.

MATERIALS

All that we have seen thus far has a bearing on the choice and use of materials. If a man is spiritual, sympathetic, and intelligent, he is able to employ the Scriptures and other materials—notably the words of prayer—as God-given means for expressing the desires of stricken hearts and as the channels for bringing comfort from on high. However brief and simple, the funeral services ought to be worthy of note for helpfulness.

In the pastor's study the materials for an approaching service may be arranged like pieces of lumber in a merchant's yard. But in the hands of a minister with a definite purpose they should be joined together for the glory of God and the solace of his children. Sometimes there is singing. Again there is a stanza or two of a poem. But the chief reliance, under God, is on the reading of the Scriptures and the words of prayer.

Ofttimes the question is where to find the materials for the coming funeral. If the minister is forehanded he has many such things ready for use. In his files or somewhere else he has them classified, so that any needed item is available at once. In the hands of a bungler, a filing cabinet might do more harm than good. But if a man has piety and brains enough to be in charge of a funeral, he will be able to use mechanical helps without becoming their slave. At best such things are secondary.

The time to begin making ready for unexpected funeral calls may be during the slack season in midsummer. In fact, such preparations ought to start while a man is in the seminary. As a help in getting under way a student may resort to books. But the most helpful materials, as a rule, are those that a man discovers for himself, preferably in the original settings. Not only do they mean much to the finder's soul; they also lend themselves readily to his needs as a pastor.

If a man has the shepherd heart he enjoys these hours of

preparation for pastoral leadership. During the early summer, when sickness is somewhat rare, he may be getting ready for funerals that are sure to come. In his files there may be a growing number of cards with texts for such occasions. There should be passages appropriate for the funeral of a child, or of an aged saint. Even if there never is an opportunity to employ some of these texts, the work of compiling them is good for a man's soul.

Much the same suggestion applies to hymns, poems, and illustrations, as well as words of prayer. Whenever a man runs across anything precious he can store it in his treasure chest. Ten years later one of these items may be a very present help in trouble. It is better to have abundance of materials that one does not need than to feel desperate because certain materials are not at hand. In short, the pastor should be able to bring out from his treasure chest things new and old.

EXPRESSION

If a minister has these other qualities he probably knows how to speak in public. The pastor who thinks clearly articulates distinctly. As an educated man, he is able to voice thoughts and feelings with clarity and interest. There may also be a touch of beauty. Hence the clergyman may choose as a motto a few words from the Prophet Isaiah: "The Lord God hath given me the tongue of the learned, that I should know how to speak" (Isa. 50: 4).

The emphasis just now is on public address as well as mastery of written words. People today are accustomed to hearing over the radio diction that is correct and pleasing. They are beginning to insist that the local clergyman use the King's English for the glory of God. Just as thoughtful folk do not listen long to the radio speaker who lacks signs of culture, so do they prefer the local minister who is a master of public speech.

Later we shall consider the purpose of the Scripture read-

ings, as well as the content of the funeral sermon. At present
the stress is on the form of all these utterances. Spiritually,
the value lies mainly in the substance of what is spoken.
Practically, the effectiveness is due more largely to the literary
form and the vocal expression. In reading the Bible the pastor
should bring out the meaning and the beauty. If he chooses
to read the short opening prayer, he should call no attention
to himself or to the fact that he is using words drawn from a
well of living English, pure and undefiled.

At a funeral the chief test of the minister's ability to speak
comes in the pastoral prayer. While never long, it should include much. There ought to be a modest pattern. The words
should be clear and pleasing. The sentences should flow.
With no evidence of nervousness or tension, the man who is
leading others to the throne of grace should be uttering words
that are full of Christian feeling. According to psychology,
when a man's heart is moved his words flow in rhythmical
beauty. Such a spirit of prayerfulness should communicate
itself to the people. When the minister is leading, everyone
should pray.

If there is a sermon, short and simple, it should be a
blending of Biblical thought and pastoral feeling. If there is
little time to prepare, the man who spends many waking hours
in working with words should be able to use them for the
glory of the God from whom they come. The fact that he
prepares whenever he can ought to encourage him to speak
with holy boldness whenever there is need of a message from
the God of all comfort and grace.

SELF-CONTROL

Equally apparent is the need of self-control. At a deathbed
or a funeral service, when everyone else may be nervous and
distraught, the minister should be calm and dependable.
When no one else seems to be certain what to do, the pastor
should know what the Lord requires of a leader. He should

have such poise and self-possession that his quiet confidence will become infectious. Erelong people should begin to say of him, lovingly: "He never loses his head. He never does or says anything not in keeping with the spirit of the hour."

Self-mastery appears in the conduct of every funeral. Into the home or funeral parlor the minister can come without calling attention to his entrance. He is able to sit still as long as he should remain seated. When at last the mortician indicates that the time has come for the minister to take charge, he moves slowly. He speaks in tones that are low but clearly audible. He controls his voice, as well as his tears. At times they may be near the surface, but they must not flow. Even if others break down and weep, this man's heart is fixed on God. Nothing on earth can disturb the poise of the ideal pastor.

Above all is self-control imperative in an emergency. No man has any more powers of leadership than he is able to use in a moment of crisis. If a surgeon is worthy to perform an operation, he knows what to do when the chief assistant faints or when the hospital catches fire. So should it be with the minister.

Once in a rural district of Oklahoma the funeral procession was fording a creek, because the recent floods had swept away the bridge. In the midst of the stream the rear axle of the hearse gave way. The man in charge commandeered a passing wagon, placed the casket in it, then led the procession to the cemetery. To the young minister officiating at one of his first funerals such resourcefulness was an object lesson of how to meet an emergency. On the way home that afternoon he prayed that he might be granted like wisdom to act in any crisis.

PRESTIGE

The last quality of which we shall think is prestige. Such a suggestion may seem strange. Should the minister of the Gospel think about his local reputation? No, not selfishly.

But neither should he forget that he represents God and the Church. When the clergyman first comes into the community he is accepted, temporarily, for the sake of the institution he serves. In a few months he will have to stand on his own feet.

Sooner or later a minister is likely to receive all the honor he deserves. Sometimes God's people do not appreciate a pastor until he has gone away, perhaps to glory. Occasionally they think more highly of a man than the facts warrant. But as a rule you can rely on the judgment of godly people when they revere a certain minister and hold aloof from another. In the time of grief they long for the guidance of a friend who has journeyed far into the King's country. They know that he can lead them close to the heart of God.

From this point of view a pastorate may be too short. On other grounds it may be wise for a man to move after four or five years. On the contrary, when people have to walk through the valley of the shadow where they bid farewell to one whom they love, they wish to receive comfort from a trusted friend. "A stranger will they not follow, but will flee from him: for they know not the voice of strangers" (John 10: 5). The minister to whom their hearts go out with longing is the one who in other days has led them safely through the dark valley.

Nonetheless, if the new pastor knows how to visit the sick and how to conduct a funeral, he can quickly win for himself a place in the hearts of the congregation. The fact that he trusts the Lord and loves people, one by one, will help to bridge every gap. After they have been with him at his first funeral, and at his first celebration of the Lord's Supper, they will know that he is a man of God.

Every minister has some sort of reputation, locally. Why should it not be worthy? Why should not his new friends thank God for sending a leader who is master of his calling? Such a man has a heart as well as a head. He knows. He cares. He is able to do the will of God on any occasion. In all the afflictions of his friends he too is afflicted. He is God's messenger of mercy.

In short, the funeral service is probably the chief test of a man's helpfulness as a pastor. For a living object lesson of such prestige, won by ceaseless toil, read *Ian Maclaren, the Life of John Watson,* by Sir William Robertson Nicoll. Over in Liverpool for years John Watson was a beloved pastor. Both as a preacher and as a writer he won distinction. To the world at large he became known as the author of *Beside the Bonnie Brier Bush* and other tales of rural Scotland. But in the eyes of those who knew him best and loved him most, John Watson was supreme as a pastor. He excelled as a comforter in the hour of grief.

There is a popular impression that a shepherd of souls is born, not made. But it was not so with John Watson. Under God, that man became a helpful pastor. Little by little he transformed himself into a messenger of mercy. Never did he find the work easy, perhaps because he was not of the outgoing temperament. Instead of starting on his afternoon rounds with joy, often he would have preferred to tarry at home and read. Some households he hesitated to enter. Certain people he did not easily like.

By faith and patience the man called of God to be a pastor rose above his personal handicaps. He learned how to employ all his gifts and graces in the service of people, especially anyone in sorrow. Throughout his home city and far beyond he became like the shadow of a great rock in a weary land. In such an achievement there is nothing magical. Rather is there a triumph of faith and perseverance.

Many a humble pastor has learned how to be helpful at all times, and especially at a funeral. His name never appears in books but it is known in heaven. His experience is heartening to other ministers. It shows that the one called of God can become worthy to wear the mantle of a Christian shepherd. Earth has no higher honor. Of any such clergyman it might be written, as of Goldsmith's "village parson": "Allured to brighter worlds, . . . [he] led the way."

Inspirational Readings

Adams, Hampton, *Pastoral Ministry*. The Cokesbury Press, 1932.
Jefferson, Charles Edward, *The Minister as Shepherd*. T. Y. Crowell
    Company, 1912.

III. The Dying Friend

IF A friend is dying, what should the pastor do? How quickly should he respond to the call? How should he deal with the doctor, the hospital authorities, the nurse? How should he greet the members of the family? How enter the room of the dying friend? Once there, what should he do and say? How long should he tarry? If the friend rallies, and lingers on in the flesh for weeks, how often should the minister call? At what hour of the day or night? After the last expiring breath, what should he do and say?

These questions may not loom so large now as in grandfather's day. In many circles then it was the custom to summon the minister whenever death seemed near. On his arrival he felt that he knew what to do and say. Sometimes his course of treatment was heroic. Occasionally it ran counter to present-day ideas of Christian kindness. That may be one reason why the pastor today does not often minister at a deathbed.

However, such experiences do come. As a minister gets older, if people discover that he has a message from the heart of God, they wish him to be present when death is drawing near to one whom they love. Whether these calls be many or few, in each case there is an appeal to the pastor's heart. The first time or two he may have a feeling akin to terror. But if he keeps his emotions under control, and simply tries to be helpful, spiritually, as a Christian friend, he will gain confidence in the Lord's power to use him as a messenger of comfort. This is no small part of what it means to be a physician of souls.

THE BASIC CREED

What a minister does at the deathbed depends much on what he believes. In the case of a godly man or woman, the pastor may stress the thought of heaven as home. If the dying friend is not a Christian, there may be more about Christ and the Cross. The underlying assumption at present is that God can save any sinner, even if death is drawing near. While such experiences are rare, the writer has witnessed a few conversions which seemed as real as that of the dying thief (Luke 23: 39-43).

In the old-time hymn "There Is a Fountain Filled with Blood," many of us shrink from the figure in the opening stanza. But in the song as a whole we find the truth of God's redeeming grace, as revealed in the Cross:

> "The dying thief rejoiced to see
> That fountain in his day;
> And there may I, as vile as he,
> Wash all my sins away."

A case will throw light on the matter of deathbed repentance. One night a young minister responded to the call of a dying stranger, an aged Scotsman. What occurred in the humble upper room was substantially as follows: The dying man whispered: "Dominie, I want to get in." The pastor thought the stranger referred to the Brotherhood of St. Andrew. "No, I want to go hame." Again the minister did not understand. He supposed that the other man's mind was wandering and that he wished to cross the ocean. But at length the stranger made it clear that he wanted to find the way back to his mother's God.

The clergyman told the dying man about the beauty of our Saviour's life and the simplicity of his teachings. But the hearer protested, feebly: "No, dominie, I'm dying, and I need the Saviour!" At last the minister forgot about his up-to-date ethical culture and started to tell the old, old story of the Cross. He spoke about the love of God for the weakest and worst of men, about the death of Christ, about the pardon of sins, and the cleansing from their guilty stains.

"That's it! That's what I need!" said the stranger. "But does it mean a mon like me?" Then the minister quoted in part the most blessed of all our evangelistic hymns:

> "Just as I am, without one plea,
> But that thy blood was shed for me."

After a while the aged Scotsman breathed his last. On the way home that night the minister felt as though he were treading on air. He was sure that he had witnessed the birth of a soul. At the same time the clergyman had found his own way back to the Cross.

In a sense this type of conversion is sudden. But on second thought it seems to be only the turning of the wandering child back to the God of mother and father. Whatever the explanation in terms of psychology, the Christian minister should have a message for a wicked man who is close to death. If the Christ of the Cross could save the penitent thief, is there any limit now to the grace of God?

> "Dear dying Lamb, thy precious blood
> Shall never lose its power
> Till all the ransomed Church of God
> Be saved, to sin no more."

THE SUMMONS

Let us turn to details, some of which are by no means spectacular. In the work of the pastorate there is far more drudgery than drama. When there is a call to a deathbed, it may not be convenient to drop everything else and respond at once, but that is the path of duty. The minister should be as alert and prompt as the family physician.

Like the weary doctor, the clergyman occasionally responds to a false alarm. Instead of a dying friend there may be only a case of hysterics. Almost every pastor

of middle age has had the experience of being awakened out
of sleep and hastening to a home to prepare for death a
person who proved not to be critically ill. Nevertheless, the
rule is to go at once, and that graciously. The minister
should thank God that the people wish him to be with them
in trouble, whether it be real or imaginary.

The call is likely to come from a hospital. There the
minister should co-operate with those in charge. He should
previously have established friendly relations with the superintendent and the office force. If at other times he has
deferred to their way of doing things, they will help him
when he comes to minister at a deathbed. With few exceptions these friends are religiously minded. They soon learn
to trust the minister who knows how to deal with sickness
and death.

In an emergency case the minister has the right of way.
Ordinarily he secures permission from the doctor before
calling on one of his patients who is critically ill. But the
hospital authorities know when to waive formalities. As
soon as the minister arrives at the office someone escorts him
to the sick chamber. On the way he learns as much as he can
about the case. Especially does he wish to know if the friend
seems to be conscious and if the end appears to be imminent.

Within the room the pastor moves and acts quietly. He
knows that a sick person is sensitive to new noises and that
anything sudden may cause a shock. On the other hand, the
minister should be natural. He ought never to walk on tiptoe
or speak in a sepulchral tone. He should not look funereal
or afraid. Without glancing to the right or the left, he should
go to the bedside. There he may kneel, or else be seated,
if there is a waiting chair. He should not bend over the patient. If the friend holds out his hand, the minister takes it,
but scarcely otherwise.

If the sick person is conscious, and is not breathing his last,
there may be a few moments of silence. The pastor is waiting
for a whisper. When there is no word, he may ask, gently and

slowly, if there is anything for which he should pray. In any case there is a brief word from the Scriptures, such as Matt. 11: 28-30, and a short prayer. Both the passage from the Bible and the prayer should be spoken, not read. If there is no immediate crisis, it may be expedient to repeat the Apostles' Creed. But as a rule that would involve too much of a strain. It is usually better to close with The Lord's Prayer, uttered deliberately, and then pronounce the benediction.

If every moment seems likely to be the last, take less time. Get at once to the heart of the Gospel. Over in England when Bishop J. Taylor Smith was chaplain general he had a final test for each ministerial applicant: "I am dying. In a few words tell me what I must do to be saved." What appeal could be more vital, and more difficult? Here is one way of speaking. It assumes that the dying man is conscious, somewhat familiar with Christian truth, and aware of his approaching end:

"My brother, God is your Father; he loves you. Christ is your Friend; he died for you. Only his Cross can save us sinners. 'If we confess our sins, he is faithful and just to forgive us our sins' (I John 1: 9). Do you want me to pray for you?" If so, there are a few simple petitions, based on God's promises of forgiveness. There is time for only one truth, the pardoning love of God, made known in the Cross. There is need of only one response, with which the prayer may close. From his heart the dying man should say with the minister a portion of the old hymn, especially one stanza:

> " 'Just as I am! Thou wilt receive,
>   Wilt welcome, pardon, cleanse, relieve;
>   Because thy promise I believe,
>   O Lamb of God, I come!' "

However short the time, be sure to speak slowly. If the words must be few, still they ought to be clear. In case the dying man seems not to be conscious, speak as though he were able to follow every word. Especially in the case of a paralytic stroke, although there may be no evidence that the patient is aware of what is going on about him, the pastor may find that his few words have touched the heart and that there is meaning in the pressure of the hand.

As a rule, however, such moments are more helpful to the members of the family circle than to the one who is dying. If only for their sakes, the pastor should be careful about what verse of Scripture he quotes and what other forms of worship he employs. Especially if they are from Scotland, he may repeat part of a psalm, notably the Twenty-third. Many a golden passage he ought to know by heart, word for word. If the people attach value to symbolism, he may put his hand on the forehead while pronouncing the benediction. Whatever the procedure, it should center round the dying friend.

In a home there is usually less routine than in a hospital. If a nurse is in charge, a few words with her outside the door will help to guide the clergyman. However, there should be no whispering where the patient will hear, and feel that he is the subject of conversation. Within the room the minister speaks to no one save the dying man. It is easier to do that aright if few others are present. Indeed, a deathbed confession should be made in private. Everyone should leave the dying one alone with the pastor and his God. In a rural community, however, a suggestion that the members of the family retire might be counted an affront.

An illustrative case will show what not to do at a deathbed. The writer's first experience was with a family who belonged to a neighboring congregation. Their minister, who was out of town for the day, had until recent years been a blacksmith. While he knew nothing about school and little about books, he had accumulated a wealth of practical wisdom. In circumstances less awesome the contrast between him and the young graduate of university and seminary would have been ludicrous.

When the young man arrived at the house he was stiff with fright. He found the large front room downstairs filled with curious neighbors. On the bed in the far corner lay the aged father. His every gasp seemed likely to be his last. The death rattle had already begun to sound. On the table near the door, fifteen feet from the bed, was a lighted oil lamp. Taking his station there, the young minister began to read the Ninetieth Psalm, as at a funeral service.

Before he had gone far with his formalism, there was a stir near the door. The people opened up the way for the older minister to come through. Going at once to the bed, he knelt there and commenced to pray. In a few words, slow and clear, but not loud, he committed the unconscious man to the keeping of the Father God. Then this older minister pronounced the benediction. Someone brought him a chair. Without looking to the right or left, there he sat, watching the face of the dying man. Erelong came the end. Rising to his feet, the pastor spoke quietly to his assembled neighbors, suggesting that they retire so that he could be alone with the members of the family.

Meanwhile, fortunately, everyone had forgotten about the young clergyman. As soon as the pastor arrived, the young brother had taken refuge in silence. During the next minutes he learned from an untutored lay preacher certain lessons that someone might have taught back in the seminary. To this day the "educated" minister wonders why he and his classmates were ordained to the ministry without having served some sort of apprenticeship. On the other hand, he knows that in many a situation the pastor must rely upon God and thus meet the unexpected without fear.

THE LINGERING ILLNESS

The case reported above was exceptional. In fact, our books may give the impression that the pastoral ministry is largely a succession of crises, whereas it is chiefly a matter of routine. For instance, an elderly woman has a way of hanging on to life long after the end seems to be at hand. If the patient lingers at death's door for weeks, how often should the pastor call? Whenever he is in doubt, probably he should go. In no other way can he invest time and energy more profitably than in unremitting devotion to one who is dying by degrees.

Even in a large parish the writer made it his rule to call on a dying member once a day. Whenever the minister could do so, he planned to go each time at the same hour; for example, in the hospital, probably at five thirty in the afternoon; in the home, perhaps at nine thirty at night. In a hospital, the latter time would not be convenient for the nurses.

Whatever the hour, as a rule the call should be short. In days to come the family will remember the number of visits, not their length, unless the minister stays too long. If there is a special reason for his lingering, he lets the claims of the dying one have precedence. Ordinarily, it is best for the patient that the pastor come in quietly and steal out soon. At the bedside he may kneel, and there wait, in silence. This brief time should be precious. If there is anything on the heart of the dying one, what he whispers will guide the minister as he prays.

At each call, if the way be clear, there should be a verse of Scripture, spoken from the heart, and not read from a book, unless it is the patient's Bible. Some one verse may be especially fitting with the same person day after day. If so, there may also be a new word from God each time. The verse should be short, simple, and easy for the friend to recall. If at times he cannot sleep, the few words from the Book should keep singing in his soul. They are more likely to do so if they form the basis of the prayer. It too should be brief, and the rate of speech deliberate. When a patient is weak in body he is scarcely able to think fast or long. Especially in repeating The Lord's Prayer, the minister should speak so deliberately that the patient can join, at least in his heart.

On successive days there should be different forms of benediction. Fortunately, the Bible has various words of blessing.

The following case is somewhat typical. Dr. X., fifty years of age, was dying at his home with inoperable cancer. He knew that he had not long to live. All through the day he kept looking forward to nine thirty, when he knew that the minister would call. If there was a church meeting, the hour might be a little later. In that case the minister would explain the matter the night before. After the call, if the patient could not sleep, he would keep saying to himself whatever he remembered most clearly: a verse of Scripture, a sentence from the prayer, or a stanza of a hymn. In selecting these materials the pastor aimed to leave something easy to recall.

From such visits to an upper room the minister often receives far more than he gives. He learns afresh the meaning of human pain, and Christian courage, as well as divine grace. In his autobiography George A. Gordon, of Boston, tells of lessons that he learned at a bedside in Maine during his first pastorate. A gentlewoman of early middle age was wasting away with tuberculosis. Three times a week he talked with her about life and death, the Judgment Day, and the life everlasting. One night when the thermometer was thirty degrees below zero he was summoned to her deathbed. As long as he lived he thanked God for those revelations in the upper room, where the dying friend brought her young pastor near to the heart of God.

Such experiences cause a man to know his Bible and his hymnbook as never before. He has a new incentive for intercessory prayer. As his heart becomes filled with the Spirit of God there is new power and radiance in the pastor's everyday life. In the pulpit also there is a new note of triumph. The older people thank God and say one to another: "What has come over our minister? He preaches and prays better than ever before." The answer is that he has found at the bedside of a dying friend the inner meaning and the glory of the Christian religion.

In an occasional experience there is need of rare wisdom
and tact. For instance, there is the case of Mrs. G. At the
hospital, after an operation for cancer, this woman of middle
age was dying. Despite the fact that she was a devoted Christian, her pastor insisted on conducting daily inquisitions into
the state of her soul. One afternoon he stayed so long that
the nurse asked him to leave. The patient was wrought up
nervously. That night she could not sleep. Her physician, not
a churchman, was furious. He forbade the pastor to return.
The next morning the husband requested another minister
to call on the dying woman.

This clergyman, being new in the town, consulted with his
senior elder, who advised him to go and not to confer with
the pastor. (The latter part of the advice seems to have been
an error in judgment.) The physician, when approached by
the husband, reluctantly gave his consent for a single call,
not to exceed three minutes. After it was over he sent word
to the new minister, "You can see any of my patients whenever you desire." Through this doctor, as well as the nurses,
the report went round. Henceforth that minister had free
access to almost any sickroom he wished to visit.

It is seldom wise or necessary to call on a person who belongs to another parish. In the case before us the lay adviser knew all the parties concerned. He felt that the new
minister should give the needs of the dying woman precedence over ministerial etiquette. A few days later he advised
that the minister who had brought her comfort should accept
the invitation to conduct the funeral services. Meanwhile the
family as a whole had severed all connection with the church
whose pastor had tried to dangle their dear mother over the
bottomless pit. Doubtless he was a good man, but he was not
a wise pastor.

THE DEATHBED CONFESSION

The following case is still more delicate. The facts are dis-
guised, because the author agrees with Dr. R. C. Cabot, in

The Art of Ministering to the Sick: "Don't preach about the sick, or repeat stories about them. Like the doctor, the minister hears confidences and becomes conversant with many secrets. Some of them would make admirable illustrations. Most of them feed people's idle curiosity about their neighbors. People soon find out who keeps confidences and who does not. We believe that a minister's experiences with the sick should enrich his sermons, as all experience does, but this need involve no violations of confidence, and no anonymous stories. They are sure to be recognized."

John Doe, sixty years of age, was a victim of pernicious anemia. Despite repeated transfusions of blood, he was dying. Erelong he was likely to lapse into unconsciousness. This he learned one afternoon from the physician, whose business it is to inform the patient about the probable course of his disease. That evening when the minister called, the dying man asked his wife and the nurse to leave the room. A little later, with tears in his eyes, he whispered, "Will God pardon me for my sins of long ago?" Then he explained as much as the pastor needed to know.

The minister was shocked. He had been preaching much about the forgiveness of sins, but seldom with reference to a member of the church, a man of repute in the community. To hear this friend confessing his sins made the pastor shudder. Fortunately, he had the grace to keep silent until he knew what he should say. Without referring to the facts in the case, and without showing how he had felt at first, he quoted slowly a few texts, which his friend had often heard in the sanctuary:

"Come now, and let us reason together, saith the Lord: though your sins be as scarlet, they shall be as white as snow" (Isa. 1: 18). "If we confess our sins, he is faithful and just to forgive us our sins, and to cleanse us from all unrighteousness. . . . The blood of Jesus Christ his Son cleanseth us from all sin" (I John 1: 9, 7). Then the minister spoke to his friend by his Christian name: "John, are you sincerely sorry for the sins that you have confessed, and all others that you have committed? Trusting solely in the merits of Christ and his Cross, do you now receive God's pardon and his cleansing grace?"

To each question the dying man whispered, eagerly, "Yes!" The minister, knowing him to be a man of his word, formally assured him that his sins had been forgiven. In fact, they had probably been pardoned years before. But they had left on the conscience such a stain that he found it difficult to be sure of God's redeeming mercy. If there had been time and strength it would have been fitting for him to receive the Sacrament. At any rate, through the official representative of God and the Church that penitent received assurance of pardon and peace.

No two cases are alike. If that man's disease had been farther advanced, it would not have been wise to keep him listening so long. The conversation required perhaps six or eight minutes. On the other hand, the easing of his conscience had a tonic effect. As for administering the Sacrament, the writer would do that only when the members of the family make the request. Even then he would consult with the physician. Ordinarily the individual Communion set is for use with the shut-in friends who are not critically ill. As a rule it is not necessary to administer the Sacrament at a deathbed.

THE SYMPATHETIC PASTOR

There are scarcely any rules about ministering to the dying. When the clergyman enters a home where death is near he almost never knows what he will find. But the Lord knows and he will guide his servant who trusts and obeys. At the deathbed the loving heart knows what to do and say. In fact, the pastor may do almost nothing. He may keep quiet. When he has nothing to say, he says it. Silence may be golden.

For years a minister felt that he had failed at a certain

deathbed. Being at the time without pastoral experience, he
had not known what to do or say. He had simply sat by the
bedside and waited with the dying friend and his wife. In
later years he learned from the widow that she had always
cherished the recollection of the way he had led her husband
down through the valley of the deepening shadows. Especially did she appreciate the minister's tactfulness in keeping
silent. Somehow he had made it clear that he cared, and
that God cared vastly more.

In a sense the main service that the minister renders is in
being with his people when they need him most. In the room
with the one who is dying, the pastor gives heed only to
him. If the last moment is approaching, the minister stays.
Usually he tarries at the bedside. But it may be more convenient for the nurse to have him wait in an adjoining room.
If he has pressing duties elsewhere he informs the nurse how
she can reach him by telephone, and then he steals away.

Why all this solicitude? One reason is that the minister
represents Christ and the Church. Another is that in the
presence of death some people expect unusual attention from
their pastor. If he is sympathetic and untiring they will love
him as long as he lives. If he seems disinterested and neglect-
ful he will lose their esteem. However, they should remember that he has countless obligations and that his time is
precious. If people love their pastor they are almost always
reasonable in their demands on his time and strength.

Concern about the deathbed has much to do with the
minister's preparations for the funeral service. In his mind
and heart, at least unconsciously, he begins to make ready
before the hour of his friend's demise. In each of the cases
reported above there was no difficulty in deciding what to
do and say at the services of farewell. Rather was there a
feeling of thankfulness because everything was right between
the friend and God. There was also a sense of relief because
the hours of pain and weakness were at an end. Hence the
memorial services could be radiant with the joy and the hope

that God alone can give and the world can never take away.

In short, the minister should be much concerned about the person who is dying, and about those whom he loves. If the pastor feels at home in the upper room where a child of the King is breathing his last, the same spirit of trust in God will carry over into the funeral service. If any minister, therefore, longs to excel in this vital part of his work, let him resolve to become a good shepherd.

At the end of the chapter are a few pages that show how clergymen of various beliefs quote a word from the Book and pray in the presence of approaching death, or else after it has come. The last few examples have to do with a child's going home to God. Through study of these texts and prayers, and countless others like them, any pastor can learn much about the theory of ministering at the bedside of a dying friend. But when the call actually comes, leave at home the funeral source book. At the deathbed speak to God out of a heart that overflows.

"Depart out of this world, O Christian soul, trusting in the name of God the Father Almighty, who created thee;
  In the name of Jesus Christ, who redeemed thee;
  In the name of the Holy Ghost, who sanctifieth thee.
  May thy rest this day (or night) be in peace, and thy dwelling-place ever be in the Paradise of God.   Amen."

FOR USE IN THE SICKROOM

Be still, and know that I am God. Ps. 46:10.

Fear not: for I am with thee. Isa. 43:5.

Why are ye so fearful? how is it that ye have no faith? Mark 4:40.

There is no fear in love; but perfect love casteth out fear. I John 4:18.

What time I am afraid, I will trust in thee. Ps. 56:3.

I will trust, and not be afraid. Isa. 12:2.

I will fear no evil: for thou art with me. Ps. 23:4.

The Lord is my shepherd; I shall not want. Ps. 23:1.

God be merciful to me a sinner. Luke 18:13.

Though your sins be as scarlet, they shall be as white as snow. Isa. 1:18.

The blood of Jesus Christ his Son cleanseth us from all sin. I John 1:7.

Him that cometh to me I will in no wise cast out. John 6:37.

Believe on the Lord Jesus Christ, and thou shalt be saved. Acts 16:31.

Lord, I believe; help thou mine unbelief. Mark 9:24.

In quietness and in confidence shall be your strength. Isa. 30:15.

As one whom his mother comforteth, so will I comfort you. Isa. 66:13.

Rejoice in the Lord alway: and again I say, Rejoice. Phil. 4:4.

Blessed are the pure in heart: for they shall see God. Matt. 5:8.

All things, whatsoever ye shall ask in prayer, believing, ye shall receive. Matt. 21:22.

Come unto me, all ye that labour and are heavy laden, and I will give you rest. Matt. 11:28.

Thou wilt keep him in perfect peace, whose mind is stayed on thee: because he trusteth in thee. Isa. 26:3.

I sought the Lord, and he heard me, and delivered me from all my fears. Ps. 34:4.

Also Ps. 4:8; 23:6; Isa. 43:2; John 14:27; Rom. 8:28; 8:32; Phil. 4:6, 7; I John 1:9; Rev. 3:20; 21:4.

❦ ❦ ❦ ❦

Most merciful Father, look graciously upon this Thy servant in *his* sore distress. Through the precious blood of Christ cleanse *him* from all sin; visit *him* with Thy salvation, and sustain *him* by Thy tender love. Grant *him* the assurance of the Saviour's presence, so that by laying hold of the hand which was pierced *he* may be led into Thine everlasting light. O Lord, in Thy mercy receive *him*. Into Thy hands we commend *his* spirit. Keep *him* safe forevermore, through the merits of Christ our Redeemer. Amen.

❦ ❦ ❦ ❦

O Lord our God, Thou alone hast the issues of life and death. Look in mercy upon this our *brother* who lies upon a bed of weakness and pain. Grant *him* the grace to repent for all *his* sins, and to rest upon Jesus Christ as Saviour and Lord.

When Thou hast finished Thy plan for *him* here on earth, give *him* an abundant entrance into Thy heavenly home, that *he* may ever serve Thee in fullness of joy, through Jesus Christ, our Lord. Amen.

❦ ❦ ❦ ❦

Merciful Father, we commend unto Thee the soul of Thy servant, that *he* may die unto this world and live unto Thee. Whatsoever sins *he* has committed we implore Thee to pardon. Whatsoever stains *he* has acquired we beseech Thee to wash away, through the cleansing power of Thy Holy Spirit. Amen.

❦ ❦ ❦ ❦

Holy Father, Thou dost not desire the death of any sinner. Here is one of Thy servants who needs Thy forgiving love. Look upon *him* in mercy. Set *him* free from sin. Prepare *him* for the life everlasting with Thee in Thy heavenly home, through Christ our Saviour. Amen.

❦ ❦ ❦ ❦

O Lord our God, Thou dost hold all souls in life and in death. Thou hast spared this our friend through long and gracious years. Receive our thanks for all Thy gifts on *him* bestowed. Grant *him* an entrance into the house not made with hands. There *he* shall serve Thee with powers equal to *his* tasks, through Jesus Christ *his* King. Amen.

✤ ✤ ✤ ✤

Grant, O Lord, faith and courage to these Thy servants who have said farewell to their beloved *brother*. Give them strength and courage for the days to come. Forbid that they should sorrow as those who have no hope. Enable them to live in the assurance of a family reunion in the Father's home, through the merits of Jesus Christ. Amen.

✤ ✤ ✤ ✤

O Lord Jesus, who didst weep at the tomb of Lazarus, Thou dost love Thy friends in this family circle. Assure them of Thy presence and comfort them in their grief. Show them that all things are working together for their good and for Thy glory. Guide them by Thy Spirit while they live and afterward receive them into glory. There they shall sing praises unto Thee, the Redeemer, with the heavenly Father and the Holy Spirit. Amen.

✤ ✤ ✤ ✤

Our heavenly Father, we beseech Thee to solace Thy children in their sorrow. As Thou didst send Thy Holy Spirit to be the Comforter of Thy people, strengthen them by His gracious indwelling, that they may be enabled to contemplate the joy of that better home where Thou art seen and worshiped in the light of all whom Thou keepest in Thine everlasting love, through Jesus Christ our Lord. Amen.

[From the Ritual of the Methodist Church, 1940.]

✤ ✤ ✤ ✤

O our God, we beseech Thee, by that love which brought
Thy Son from heaven, have compassion on the soul of this Thy
servant: forgive *him* all *his* sins and failings, and supply all
his defects. Let *him* now experience the multitude of Thy
tender mercies, and be sensible how good a God Thou art.
Grant *him*, we implore Thee, true patience and perfect resignation in *his* pains and anguish. Confirm *his* faith, strengthen
his hope, and perfect *his* charity that, departing hence, *his* soul
may be received into Thy mercy, through Jesus Christ our
Lord. Amen.

[From the Office of the Roman Catholic Church.]

☙ ☙ ☙ ☙

O blessed Redeemer, by that distress which Thou didst suffer
on the Cross, when Thou didst cry out to Thine Eternal Father,
show mercy to this Thy servant in *his* extremity; hear the desires
and petitions of *his* heart; and since *he* cannot speak for *himself*, intercede Thou for *him*, we implore Thee, for Thou art
the Eternal Word, and the Father will refuse Thee nothing.

Let those hands, which once were nailed to the Cross, now
plead for *him*, and, obtaining *his* pardon, conduct *him* into
Thine everlasting rest. Amen.

[From the Office of the Roman Catholic Church.]

☙ ☙ ☙ ☙

Into Thy merciful hands, O heavenly Father, we commend
the soul of Thy servant now departing from the body. Acknowl-
edge, we humbly implore Thee, a sheep of Thine own fold, a
lamb of Thine own flock, a sinner of Thine own redeeming.
Receive *him* into the arms of Thy mercy, into the blessed realm
of everlasting peace, into the glorious estate of Thy chosen
saints in heaven.

O most merciful Saviour, that soul cannot perish which is
committed to Thy charge; receive, we beseech Thee, this spirit
in peace. Amen.

[From the Office of the Roman Catholic Church.]

☙ ☙ ☙ ☙

O God, whose most dear Son did take little children into His arms and bless them; Give us grace, we beseech Thee, to entrust the soul of this child to Thy never-failing care and love, and bring us all to Thy heavenly Kingdom; through the same Thy Son, Jesus Christ our Lord. Amen.

[From *The Book of Common Prayer*, According to the Use of the Protestant Episcopal Church.]

✠ ✠ ✠ ✠

O Lord Jesus Christ, the only-begotten Son of God, who for our sakes didst become a babe in Bethlehem, we commit unto Thy loving care this child whom Thou art calling unto Thyself. Send Thy holy angel to bear *him* gently to those heavenly habitations where the souls of those who sleep in Thee have perpetual peace and joy, and fold *him* in the everlasting arms of Thine unfailing love, who livest and reignest with the Father and the Holy Ghost, one God, world without end. Amen.

[From *The Book of Common Prayer*, According to the Use of the Church of England.]

✠ ✠ ✠ ✠

O Almighty God, and merciful Father, to whom alone belong the issues of life and death, look down from heaven, we humbly beseech Thee, with the eyes of mercy upon this child, now lying upon the bed of sickness. Visit *him*, O Lord, with Thy salvation; deliver *him* in Thine appointed time from *his* bodily pain, and save *his* soul for Thy mercy's sake. If it be not Thy good pleasure to prolong *his* days on earth, receive *him* into those heavenly habitations where the souls of those who sleep in the Lord Jesus enjoy perpetual rest and felicity. Grant this, O Lord, for Thy mercy's sake, through Thy Son our Lord Jesus Christ, who liveth and reigneth with Thee and the Holy Ghost, ever one God, world without end. Amen.

[From *The Book of Common Prayer* . . . as Amended by the Presbyterian Divines . . . 1661.]

✠ ✠ ✠ ✠

Informative Readings

Balmforth, Henry, and Others, *Introduction to Pastoral Theology.*
 The Macmillan Company, 1937. Part II, Chapter V.
Bonnell, John Sutherland, *Pastoral Psychiatry.* Harper & Brothers,
 1938. (In the closing chapter note the manner of using a brief
 text.)
Cabot, Richard Clarke, and Dicks, R. L., *The Art of Ministering to
 the Sick.* The Macmillan Company, 1936.

—

IV. The Funeral Arrangements

WHEN death comes to a home the pastor may be present. If so, he tarries for a little while to give comfort. As for the practical arrangements, he may suggest that he return at an hour convenient to the family. Meanwhile they should consult with the mortician and otherwise determine what they wish to do. Both pastor and mortician will help them to carry out their plans.

As a rule the minister is not present when a death occurs. If the people are considerate they notify him almost immediately. But they have many other things on their minds. The word may reach him through some of the neighbors. In some communities, unfortunately, the notice comes only through the mortician. Practically all the plans are complete before the pastor is informed about what is expected of him as the representative of the Church.

After a minister has been in a parish for a year or two he should experience little difficulty in learning of any death among his people. If he takes care of the sick folk he will know when a certain member of the flock is about to die. If the end comes without warning there should be in the district some officer or member who will keep the pastor informed. If the work is properly organized for keeping him informed about newcomers and sick folk, the same channels will bring to the manse tidings about any death. At least that is the ideal.

Such a call takes precedence over everything else. However, the minister must be careful not to rush into any home where the people belong to another congregation. Even if they are his personal friends, courtesy suggests that he tarry at home until they have completed the arrangements with their pastor. Then one can express the sympathy of a Christian neighbor. While a call would be in order, a note of sympathy is less likely to be misinterpreted by watchful folk across the street. To these ethical matters we shall refer later. At present we are thinking about a normal situation, where there is no question about ministerial courtesy.

At the first call after a death there may not be much for the minister to do. If the neighbors report at once, he may arrive before the mortician. The ensuing call is pastoral. As a rule it should be short. The minister volunteers no advice about the approaching services. He expresses his sympathy. If he is to be in charge of the funeral he may suggest that he return at a later hour. Meantime the family can determine what they wish to do. They should understand that the mortician is in charge of everything except the religious exercises.

In an exceptional case there is much for the pastor to do at the first call. If the people seem helpless they probably need advice about things practical. The best person to counsel with them may be some wise deacon or friendly woman, whom the minister can ask to represent him and the church. Only in a case of extreme necessity should he advise the securing of any particular mortician. Neither should he have much to do with other practical details that do not concern him as the leader of worship.

Let the clergyman be a clergyman. Otherwise he may come to be known as the congregational errand boy, who is glad to render jitney services without charge. If his predecessor has been unduly accommodating it may not be easy for the new minister to confine himself within his own province. But it is always possible for a pastor to enlist others for what he has not time and strength to do himself. Then if things go wrong he personally is not to blame. If they go well, as they usually do, he should give others the credit, and be careful to express his thanks.

THE PRIVATE INTERVIEW

At a time convenient to the friends the minister calls again in the home. He confers, preferably, with one or two members of the family circle. The plans should be the result of previous consultation in the family group as a whole. But at the interview with the pastor it is easier for him to talk things over with one or two persons, perhaps the widow and the oldest son. Otherwise it might be as difficult to make specific arrangements as at a wedding rehearsal, where there are many women with many minds. Any single procedure may be proper, but in the end there can be only one way to carry out each part of the service.

Prior to the interview the mortician will have come and gone. Before he decides about the place and the time of the funeral service he should have conferred with the minister by telephone. At least that is the custom when the two are on friendly terms, as they ought to be. In matters relating to funerals the minister defers to the mortician as an expert in his art. As for morticians of the baser sort, the writer has had little experience. Those of the profession whom he has known best have been Christian gentlemen. Each of them has been glad to co-operate with any minister who is worthy of his calling.

In his own sphere the pastor should be as skillful and careful as the mortician. At the end of the interview now in mind, the minister should be in possession of certain facts. Obviously there are cases where some of the items below would be superfluous. Even so, it is wise to have a check list, and to keep it in mind,—if not on a card in hand,—during the interview. If it seems strange for the minister to be writing down such items, he can explain that he wishes to preserve accurate records.

Where will the services be held?
On what date? At what hour? (Repeat this to verify.)

Will the exercises be public or private?
Is any other minister to share in the services?
If so, which parts should he take?
Who is to invite the other minister?
Is any fraternal order to be present? to take part?
Is there to be music? If so, of what kind?
Who is to secure the musicians?
Is there a favorite hymn to be sung or read?
Is there a favorite text or passage of Scripture?
Is there to be a formal obituary?
If so, who will prepare it?
If the minister prepares it, what are the facts?
Where will the interment take place? Is it to be public or private?
Should the deacons arrange for extra automobiles?
Is there anything else that the church can do?
Is there any suggestion about the services?
Do the friends have the minister's telephone number?
"Is there any special request now before we pray?"

In some cases it is not easy to secure the needed information. Even at the minister's second call the people may be distraught. What do they know or care about this or that detail? They wish a service that will bring them heart's ease. Perhaps they also desire to impress the neighbors. Nevertheless, if the pastor proceeds without reference to household desires he may discover too late that he has run counter to the traditions. Within the limits of truth and good taste every family has the right to a service that will lead to abiding satisfaction.

THE OTHER MINISTER

The most delicate question may concern the desire to have another minister take part. In fact, the people may wish him to do everything. On the other hand, the pastor feels that he should be in charge, and that, since the service must be short, there should be only one leader. Such an attitude may be far from selfish. The presence of two or three clergymen tends to make a funeral service seem more human than divine. There may be more of ministerial display than heavenly comfort.

Nonetheless, the desires of the family should prevail. Since they may hesitate to offer such a suggestion, the pastor should open the way. If they inform him, hesitantly, that they wish the former minister to take practically all the service, the pastor should acquiesce, graciously. He should volunteer to communicate with the brother concerned. If the members of the family prefer to extend the invitation, they should do so in the name of the pastor. Except in an extreme case they are willing that he arrange for the services, and that he take the brief opening part himself. That is all he has a right to expect.

Occasionally the person who represents the family ignores the pastor. If so, there may be no opportunity for him to have an interview. The predecessor or some other clergyman may assume charge. In these circumstances there is little for the present minister to do, except to hold his tongue and pray for grace. At the home of sorrow he should call to express his sympathy. Perhaps he should attend the public services, and even go to the cemetery. However, if he has an engagement calling him out of town that afternoon, no one can find fault.

The writer has had no such experiences. He always found the former pastor, and other clerical brethren, eager to follow the Golden Rule. Sometimes it leads the former minister to decline the invitation. When he feels free to accept, he defers to the present pastor, even if he is young and inexperienced. In what is said during the service neither of them should refer to the other. With one accord they should strive to comfort the friends in their sorrow.

Such is the ideal. Sometimes the facts are the reverse. After a minister leaves a parish he can make his successor's pastorate a series of perplexities. Without intending to do so, the older clergyman can prevent his friends from falling in love with the younger brother, partly because his ways are different. If the two ministers are to share in a funeral service, the visiting brother may embody in his opening prayer what the young minister plans to do later in the half hour. Partly for this reason, the man in charge usually takes the opening parts himself.

In all these matters, where there may be a clash of ministerial personalities, the interests of the sorrowing friends should be paramount. If the new minister is patient and kind, even when a family here or there ignores him, gradually he should win all the favor that he deserves. Meanwhile he should resolve that by God's grace he will never seek to outshine or outwit—not to say outkick—any other clergyman. At the root of such difficulties between two ministers there is likely to be jealousy, as well as pride. Neither spirit has any place in the heart of God's servant, above all when he stands in the presence of death.

THE FINAL ARRANGEMENTS

Elsewhere we shall consider what to do when a fraternal order is to take part in the funeral services. Under normal conditions the interview we have in mind need last only fifteen or twenty minutes. When the minister has all the facts in hand he may suggest that the household assemble for a word of prayer. Or he may think it better to have brief devotions with the person who has helped to make the plans. In either case, unless the family traditions call for some other posture, it is good to pray while standing. Then one can steal away at once, and without a word, though there ought to be a firm clasping of each right hand.

The idea is to depart from the home as the pastor, not as a man of affairs. In the same spirit of prayer the minister goes to his study at the church, or else to his home. Then he sets in motion whatever is necessary to carry out the plans for the use of the church, the securing of singers, and the arranging for extra automobiles. If there is an office secretary, she can relieve the pastor of such details. If not, perhaps his wife can do the telephoning. In any case, the minister needs to check up on the final plans. Before the hour for the funeral everything should be in readiness.

Meanwhile the pastor alone can prepare for what is far more vital than all those details. He is to be in charge of the religious exercises. If he is to lead aright, he should plan to be alone with his God. There let us leave the man with the shepherd heart. The Lord bless him and use him as a means of grace to the friends who on the morrow will look to him for light in all their darkness.

"Comfort ye, comfort ye my people, saith your God. Speak to the heart of Jerusalem" (Isa. 40: 1, 2 from the Hebrew).

Practical Readings

Hathaway, Helen, *Manners*. E. P. Dutton & Co., seventh edition, 1934. Pages 138-150.

Odgers, J. Hastie, and Schutz, E. G., *The Technique of Public Worship*. Methodist Book Concern, 1928. Chapter X.

V. The Public Services

THE funeral services should be Christian throughout. What our religion calls for in any one case depends on many factors. Most of them appear in this book; some do not. The man called of God to lead must be resourceful. He should adapt means to ends. Before we turn to practical methods, let us think about the purpose. What are the reasons for holding a funeral service?

The chief aim is to glorify God. The best way to do that in the presence of death is to administer comfort. As the root idea of the word makes clear, to comfort means to strengthen in the Lord. Both in making the arrangements and in carrying them out, the pastor strives to bring the people into right relations with God, so that they will accept his plan for their altered lives.

There is need also of setting before them certain truths and ideals that will help in days to come. Hard as they may find it to accept sorrow now, they will need still more of God's sustaining power in days to come. As long as they live they should remember with thanksgiving the services that bring them close to God and persuade them one by one to lay hold on the hand that was pierced.

At times there may be an opportunity for evangelism. Certain members of the family circle may not yet be consciously and gladly children of God. Others among the throng of relatives and neighbors may be still farther from the Lord and his Church. Thus the need for the Evangel is real. But as a rule the appeal should be indirect. Within the brief limits of time allotted for the service it would be unwise to attempt much more than to comfort those that mourn and prepare them for unknown morrows.

As for the funeral services, their character will depend in part on where they are held. This matter deserves more attention than it usually receives.

THE APPOINTED PLACE

As a rule local custom goes far to determine the choice of the place for the services. In a current issue of *The New York Times* are fifty-eight death notices. Twenty-four call for services at funeral parlors; twelve, in churches, chiefly Catholic; six, in private residences. Most of the other notices indicate that the services will be in private, or else not in New York City. Needless to say, conditions there are not normal. In a small town funeral parlors would not be much in demand.

The logical place for many a funeral is in the home. That is where the deceased has lived. It has been the place dearest to his heart. The ties there are personal and enduring. Everything is familiar. The atmosphere is friendly. Amid such surroundings it should not be difficult for anyone to think of heaven as home, and of death as falling asleep at the end of life's little day. However, a funeral service may not be feasible in a tiny cottage, or a vast apartment house.

When the exercises are to be held in a Christian home it may be comparatively easy for the minister to make his plans. If the departed has been a believer in Christ, the occasion calls for uplifting worship. The spirit of the services ought to be that of Christian peace and hope. There need be nothing about "death's cold, sullen stream," or "Hark! from the tombs a doleful sound." As a rule that sound is pagan. In a Christian service of farewell why pitch the worship in a minor key?

The exercises in the home should be short. In making the plans it is good to think of twenty minutes as the upper limit. If the people desire a number of hymns, the time may

be thirty minutes. But as a rule it is not wise to keep everyone on a strain for half an hour. According to a familiar
saying about a sermon, few souls are saved after the first
twenty minutes. In a memorial service few hearts find comfort during the latter portion of a thirty-minute service.

On the other hand, there should be no haste. If the minister speaks and acts deliberately, no one will leave or fall
asleep. If he is to make a lasting impression for time and
eternity, he will need fifteen minutes or more. Whatever
the length of time, he ought to make every word count. In
such circumstances it is an almost unpardonable offense to
be loquacious. Even if there has been little opportunity for
immediate preparation, the clergyman should school himself
in speaking directly to the point.

In keeping with the spirit of the home, everything should
be simple. The appeal should be more to the heart than to
the head. The emphasis should be on the expression of
Christian feeling rather than the teaching of religious truth.
At other times and places there is a call for instruction
about the meaning of death and the assurance of everlasting
life, but just now the need is for spiritual comfort. It comes
best through uplifting worship that has to do with the living
Christ. Once he died on the cross. Some day he is coming in
glory. Meanwhile he is here in our midst. He is tender to
sympathize and mighty to save.

The appeal to the heart should be personal. However, the
feelings should be under firm control. There is not likely
to be any emotional disturbance if the minister keeps away
from personalities. If there is an obituary it should be factual
rather than laudatory. Otherwise nothing need be said directly about the deceased. There need be no mention of
any other person, except the Lord Jesus. At a Christian
service of farewell he should be all in all. In the light of his
presence the friends should find peace for the present hour
and hope for the days to come. The leader's aim, therefore,

is to bring them one by one face to face with the living Christ.

Such a time of worship ought to be beautiful. The reference here is to nothing striking or flamboyant, but rather to the sort of spiritual beauty that breathes through the Crusaders' Hymn, "Fairest Lord Jesus." In every part of the service, notably in the readings from the Bible and in the prayers, the beauty of the Lord should shine forth. If there is music, or any other added feature, it should have a beauty all its own. In making ready for a funeral service this is a wise motto: "Let the beauty of the Lord our God be upon us."

The simplest way to test words for their beauty is to repeat them aloud. If they flow along with a quiet motion, whether it be that of poetry or of prose, they are probably worthy of a place in a funeral service, but not otherwise. If the leader is a lover of the beauty that dwells in words, he is able to read them so that they will move the heart Christward. If he can read from the Book, and then speak from the heart when he prays, he will cause the friends to feel that God is near and that he is good. If the beauty of the Lord is to remain with them, it should shine forth through the leader of the service.

There is a sort of somber beauty that has little place in a Christian funeral. For example, in the Bible few books have more of rhythmical movement than certain portions of Lamentations, but they are more in keeping with the gloom of the Wailing Wall in old Jerusalem than with the spirit of the celebration when a saint goes home to God. Then if ever the Gospel is good tidings. The call is for the children of the Most High to cast the mantle of forgetfulness over the days and weeks of waiting, the hours of agony and tears, the sadness of farewell. They should learn to look upward, not down; and forward, not back.

Throughout the services there should be a sense of motion. If there is to be no evidence of haste, neither should there be any appearance of delay, or of marking time. Since there is in the leader's mind and heart only one controlling purpose, that of bringing comfort, he can keep moving on from stage to stage. Each successive part should be fairly short. But there should be no break from beginning to end. Step by step he should lead all so close to God that erelong they will be ready to receive the most beautiful of the benedictions (Num. 6: 24-26).

One reason for having a benediction at this service, with another at the grave, is that some persons will be present at one time and not at the other. A more cogent reason is that the benediction should be the crowning feature of any religious service. When the minister solemnly pronounces these words of blessing they should bring to trustful hearts the healing balm of heaven. On those who have faith to receive the divine blessing, these last few words bestow "the manifold helpfulness of the Triune God."

Even when the exercises at the home lead up to the benediction there is still a sense of incompleteness. As the friends go out from beneath the family roof they should look forward to the services at the cemetery. Beyond that they should set their hearts on the open gates of heaven. They should be thinking of the family reunion in the Father's home.

Such was the spirit that prevailed throughout the services in memory of Mrs. L. For months she had been wasting away. At last she was free from her weakness and pain. Since the interment on the morrow was to be at her old village church forty miles away, the services were held in the home at night. The house was filled with loving neighbors and friends. The season was a day or two before Christmas. At first the young minister had wondered how he could blend the beauty of yuletide with the thought of death. Then he thought to himself, "In each case the spirit is that of homegoing." Few of those present will ever forget the resulting vision of heaven in terms of Christmas Eve at home by the fireside.

THE CHURCH FUNERAL

Sometimes funeral services ought to be held in the main sanctuary. If the throng of relatives and friends is too large for the home, the logical place for the ceremony of farewell is at the church. Especially is this the case if the departed has been a lay officer or a leader in the women's work. What is the sanctuary for if not to shelter God's children in their time of sorrow as well as of joy? If the church doors are open wide for many a wedding, should they not also be open for a funeral?

The time to make these facts clear is when no member has recently died. Every once in a while, through the bulletin or in other ways, the minister can announce that the church is available for funerals as well as weddings. When there is added expense for heating the building, the members of the congregation will understand without being told. In dealing with strangers it may be necessary occasionally to fix a moderate fee. But if it is financially possible the church should be open for any funeral service, without money and without price.

When the throng is not large, a more fitting place may be the chapel. Every church of any size ought to have a small sanctuary, as beautiful as the large one, and likewise dedicated to worship. At the First Presbyterian Church in New York City the chapel is perhaps the most pleasing part of the entire edifice. At the Old First Church of Orange, New Jersey, the smaller sanctuary is known as "The House of Prayer." Either of those chapels is large enough to accommodate comfortably the normal funeral party. Such a setting is almost ideal. It is churchly without seeming cold. In the main sanctuary the people might feel lost.

It is more difficult to plan for a funeral at the church than in a home. One reason is that people expect more. Another is that the arrangements must include two places, rather than one. Some ministers make it their rule to be present at the home, with a brief service in private, before the funeral party goes to the church. That is entirely proper, if the members of the family so desire. Ordinarily it is easier for the pastor to greet them at the main entrance to the church. Thus there need be no haste in getting from the home to the sanctuary and in putting on the pulpit gown.

For ten or fifteen minutes before the funeral party is expected there may be meditative music from the organ. As the people assemble there should be no conversation in either the lobby or the pews. Above all the minister should refrain from chatting with those who enter. He does well to tarry in the study until one of the ushers notifies him that the funeral party is arriving. Without haste he should go to the front entrance. Step by step with the mortician, the minister should lead the procession toward the chancel.

All the while the organist should be playing softly. No music is more fitting than the melodies of familiar hymns about Christ and the Cross. When the procession enters the people should rise and remain standing until after the members of the family are seated. In some churches it is the custom for the minister, as he precedes the casket down the center aisle, to repeat the words of our Lord: "I am the resurrection, and the life: he that believeth in me, though he were dead, yet shall he live: And whosoever liveth and believeth in me shall never die" (John 11: 25, 26).

The members of the funeral party take the front pews reserved for them on the right. The pallbearers go to the front pews on the left. Meanwhile the minister walks to the pulpit, or other place from which he plans to conduct the service. If the funeral party is seated in front of the lectern, he may wish to stand there. From this point forward the service may follow much the same order as at a private residence.

A church funeral, however, differs from one in a home. In fact, unless the leader is a master of his art, there may be coldness and stiffness. If the sanctuary is dark by day, there should be artificial light, though not much. Where the atmosphere of the home would lead to emphasis on things personal, the spirit of the sanctuary may suggest something more churchly. This is one reason why the minister does not wear a pulpit gown in the home, but always does in the church, if that is counted proper. When there is a message, it may be about the communion of saints, both on earth and in heaven.

As a rule services in the sanctuary last a little longer than they would in a home. Even if there is singing and a sermon, it is wise to think in terms of half an hour. Still more than in a home, the appearance of haste or of undue brevity might make the occasion seem inconsequential. Within thirty minutes, however, it should be possible, ordinarily, to greet the party at the door, conduct the service as a whole, and then escort them from the sanctuary.

Before the minister goes from the church he can step into the study and remove his pulpit gown. Then he should precede the party all the way to the funeral car. The pace should be slow, not only because the occasion is solemn, but also because those in charge of the casket need time. At the funeral car the minister stands in the street, facing the rear of the hearse, and far enough away so as not to interfere with the bearers. Unless the weather is inclement or cold, his head is uncovered. However, it is proper for an elderly man to wear a skullcap.

While the members of the family are being escorted to their motor cars the minister takes his seat in the automobile appointed for him. It may belong to the mortician, who is always glad to send for the minister at his residence and later deliver him there. In such a case the pastor may ride to the cemetery with the pallbearers. Less frequently, he goes with the mortician, or the chief assistant. Occasionally, the minister rides with the bereaved family. Whatever the arrangement, it is made by the mortician. He in turn carries out the wishes of the family.

In such matters one defers to the mortician. If he thinks

that the minister should ride in a stately conveyance, that is the part of wisdom. Otherwise the pastor may prefer to use his own car, provided it is presentable. On the way home from the cemetery he can make several calls at the hospital or elsewhere. Funerals are most frequent at the time of year when illness is most prevalent. They usually come in the afternoon, which is the best time for calling.

If the people concerned know that the minister has on his heart other folk who need his tender care, they will scarcely object to slight informality. Even if they should, the responsibility for the arrangements lies with the mortician. Whatever the minister plans to do, it should be clear to the man in charge. Neither at the church nor at the cemetery should the clergyman cause any inconvenience or delay. When everything else moves according to schedule, the public representative of the Most High should be ready for each step when it is due. "Let all things be done decently and in order" (I Cor. 14: 40).

The church funeral that the writer remembers most vividly was that of Mother W. Throughout the parish for years she had been known as "the flower lady." In person she was as dainty as a rose and in life she was as fragrant. Apart from her duties at home, her chief concern was for the flowers in the sanctuary. On Sunday night or Monday morning she sent pulpit flowers to persons who were sick or in distress. Whenever there was serious illness in a home, or a church member in the hospital, she ordered, in the name of the congregation, a box of flowers or a plant in bloom. During times of convalescence she made many a cheery call.

Such a messenger of beauty may be worth more to the parish than the average assistant pastor. The flower lady was so beloved that the services in her honor had to be held in the main sanctuary. Since the interment was to be at her girlhood home far away, the time for the assembly was in the evening, as the sun was about to set. The season was early in summer, when flowers were most lovely and profuse.

From gardens near and far came such old-fashioned flowers as she had loved. They filled the front portion of the sanctuary.

During the afternoon anyone who wished to look upon the face of this dear friend could do so in the church, where she seemed to be sleeping among the roses. As the time drew near for the services the organist began to play softly the melodies of the flower lady's most beloved hymns. Erelong the casket was closed, not to be opened again in the church. Soon the pews were filled. On the way home from work the men joined with the women who had come from their homes. The spirit was that of a family reunion among those who loved each other in the Lord. Within the throng were more than a few from other congregations.

In the services the dominant note was that of beauty. The deceased had been seventy years of age. She had come to her death through a painful accident. Hence it would have been easy to stress what was dark and hard and awful. But the prevailing spirit was thanksgiving for the memories of bygone years, and rejoicing because of her going home. The readings and the prayers had to do with "mother, home, and heaven." The songs were such as she had loved to sing at home and in church. Instead of the conventional obituary there was a loving tribute prepared by the officers of the church and read by the pastor in their name.

Since the members of the family desired a brief message, it was on the words, "The beauty of the Lord our God be upon us" (Ps. 90: 17). After the services of farewell, as the people departed from the sanctuary, they loved to think of their departed friend in terms of beauty. Many of them felt that heaven was nearer than it ever had seemed before.

The order of service that appears below was prepared especially for the occasion. Although the congregation joined with the choir in singing the hymns, there was no announcement. The numbers were on the bulletin board. Since the interment was to be elsewhere, the services in the sanctuary

included a few items that usually belong at the grave. Since
the occasion was memorable, owing to the years of service
rendered by the departed, the exercises were slightly longer
than is customary.

Organ Music: Favorite Hymn Tunes

Hymn of Entreaty: "Abide with Me" . . . . *Monk*

The Reading of Psalms 103; 23

The Prayer of Adoration and Confession

Hymn of Thanksgiving: "Now Thank We All Our
God" . . . . *Crüger*

The Apostles' Creed

The New Testament Readings

Music by the Choir: "Unfold, Ye Portals" . . . *Gounod*

The Tribute Prepared by Officers of the Church

The Message by the Pastor

Hymn of Exultation: "Hark! Hark, My Soul!" . . . *Smart*

The Covenant Benediction

Organ Music: "Our Father Who Art in Heaven" . . *Bach*

THE FUNERAL PARLOR

One of the most difficult places in which to conduct a
Christian service of farewell is at a funeral parlor or cemetery chapel. Such places are doubtless essential. If present
trends continue, the majority of funerals may be held in
rooms set apart exclusively for the purpose. For that very
reason the atmosphere is likely to seem sepulchral. The associations are with death, not with life everlasting. No matter what is said or done, the services may seem hollow, if not
hopeless.

Nevertheless, it is possible to be a minister of comfort and
hope in the most conventional funeral parlor. God is there,

and he is waiting to bless all that is done for his glory. In like manner it is feasible to have a Christian burial on a battlefield by night, as the chaplain stands by the grave of a young soldier who has recently been slain. All the while everyone feels that the situation is abnormal. But by faith the servant of God can rise above his feelings.

At a funeral parlor the problem is unlike that in the home or church. There the minister would conduct a service in harmony with the loftiest traditions and ideals of the hallowed spot. It has been the scene of love and joy such as we associate with heaven. But in a funeral parlor the Christian leader must strive to foster a spirit foreign to the surroundings. The very name "parlor" suggests something conventional and stiff. It makes one think of a marriage parlor, which is a sorry place for a wedding ceremony.

Some of the up-to-date rooms for funerals are models of architecture and interior decoration. Even so, the associations are with death. Never does the place ring with the shouts of children. Never does it sound forth the bells of Christmas or the notes of the wedding march. Hence there is little to suggest the mercies of God in the past or his promises for years to come.

It may be that all this is unfair. Each man's experience is his own. As for the writer, he does not recall with satisfaction any exercises that he ever conducted or attended at a funeral parlor. He wishes that it were feasible to have every Christian service of farewell in the living room of a home or within the confines of a church.

In time, however, it should be possible to change the atmosphere of many a funeral parlor. As a rule the services there are in the hands of Christians. In the early centuries of the Church at Rome the saints filled the catacombs with emblems of Christian hope and joy. In like manner, if the minister is in close touch with the Lord, he can rise above the conventional gloom and cold formality of any funeral parlor.

The way to transform such a place is to change the temper of our funeral customs. If in days to come every Christian funeral is in keeping with our holy faith, the places set apart for such services will be suggestive of peace and joy, with many foregleams of heaven. Meanwhile the pastor can say to his sorrowing friends, as they sit in a room given over to gloom, "Lift up your hearts." A fitting response would be: "We lift them up unto the Lord."

At a funeral parlor both pastor and people should remember what a man of old learned at a spot that had seemed to him God-forsaken: "Surely the Lord is in this place; and I knew it not. . . . This is none other but the house of God, and this is the gate of heaven" (Gen. 28: 16, 17).

THE PAGAN CUSTOMS

Thus far little has been said about unseemly funeral customs. One of them is the wearing of black raiment. Wholly apart from the cost, which may be heavy, the practice is pagan. Black is suggestive of night, gloom, despair. If there must be special funeral garments, let them be white. That is a symbol of the day, of purity, and of hope. Even more laudable is the custom of putting on the best attire at hand, provided it calls no attention to itself. Fortunately, the whole matter is righting itself, and that without ministerial pressure. More and more is common sense likely to prevail.

Another reform has been still more striking. A generation or two ago the favorite time for holding a funeral was on Sunday afternoon. Now the custom is almost extinct. Except when the body is to be taken elsewhere for burial, a Sunday funeral is almost unknown. Here again, common sense has prevailed.

A third practice is gradually disappearing. It is that of letting the public services culminate with "viewing the remains." The most harrowing scenes that accompany death may occur at this juncture. As the curiosity seekers parade past the open casket, the members of the family may have to look on. How can they keep back their tears? If they desire to be alone once more with the body of their beloved, that may be their privilege. But they ought to be shielded from the gaze of the curious.

Unfortunately, in many a rural community there is little that the minister can do, at least directly. Seldom does anyone ask what he thinks about such practices. However much his soul may revolt, he should hold his peace and bide his time. As a rule reforms are more effective if they come about gradually, in response to the desires of the people concerned.

If the clergyman were so disposed he could request the official board to forbid viewing the remains after a service in the sanctuary. In more than a few churches pagan music is no longer allowed, whether at a funeral or a wedding. The same principle would apply to this other practice. It is better, however, to work slowly and indirectly. In conference with the mortician the minister can suggest a more fitting plan. Whether the services are to be held in the church or elsewhere, the neighbors who find satisfaction in such things can see the body beforehand, at a time convenient for all concerned.

However much the pastor may deplore viewing the remains, he has no right to protest unless the practice interferes with the religious exercises. He has a right to arrange that these shall culminate with the benediction and silent prayer, to be followed by gentle music from the organ.

From beginning to end everything in such farewell services ought to be in harmony with the spirit of the Christian religion. Later we shall consider what to do when the departed has not been a believer. At present we are thinking about a normal ceremony, in memory of one who has loved the Lord and the home church.

At such a time the souls of believers should be filled with thanksgiving as they recall God's mercies in the past. Their hearts ought also to be full of peace as they trust in the ever-present Saviour. Their spirits should rejoice as they look forward to a family reunion in the Father's home.

Funeral Manuals

Halsey, Jesse, *A Living Hope*. The Abingdon Press, 1932 (loose leaves).

Harmon, Nolan Bailey, Jr., *Pastor's Ideal Funeral Manual*. Abingdon-Cokesbury Press, 1942.

Leach, William Herman, *Cokesbury Funeral Manual*. The Cokesbury Press, 1932.

VI. The Homemade Ritual

EVERY pastor ought to have some sort of funeral ritual. The word, as here employed, refers to a regular way of leading in the worship of God, time after time. In general, there are two kinds of ritual: the one is prescribed by a man's Church; the other is made in the home study. The one is adopted; the other is adapted. The question about which is better does not concern us now. In describing the one that is made at home there is no desire to disparage the one that is prescribed.

The merits of the prescribed ritual are well known. The majestic cadences of the Protestant Episcopal burial service are second to nothing of the sort. The corresponding portions of the Lutheran liturgy are equally worthy of honor. More ancient than either are the burial rites of the Roman Catholic Church. With such examples of liturgical art every clergyman should be familiar. Sooner or later a minister will be asked to read the Episcopal burial service. If so, he should be able to do it with distinction.

The pastor should be still more intimately acquainted with the book of forms issued by his own denomination. In one branch of the Church the title is *The Book of Common Worship*; in another body, *The Book of Service*. Almost without exception, these volumes of late have been well edited. Each of them is in accord with the traditions and ideals of the denomination. Whenever a minister is in doubt concerning what to do and say at a funeral, he can fall back on his official book. The fact that the suggested funeral forms are somewhat general makes them fitting when it would be unwise to deal directly with the "life situation."

In many another funeral, also, the pastor can draw from
his favorite book of forms. But as the months go by he may
feel a longing for an order of his own. For instance, he may
think that the readings from the Bible should call forth
words of prayer more often than in some of the rituals that
he finds in books. If he conducts many funerals he will
tend to follow much the same order time after time. If so,
there may be no reason why he should change what he has
found most helpful to his people. But it can do no harm for
him to check up once in a while.

What, then, is the philosophy undergirding this kind of
"free worship"? The principle is that the funeral service
should employ spiritual materials in meeting human needs.
Since they are much the same from one occasion to another,
the general order may be fairly well fixed. But since in
almost every funeral certain conditions are unique, the content should vary somewhat widely. For example, at the
funeral of an aged saint who has fallen asleep after long
months of weary waiting, the readings and the prayers would
not be like those at the services over a young brakeman who
has met his death in a railroad collision.

THE PRACTICAL DIFFICULTIES

It is far from easy to make a funeral ritual of one's own.
One difficulty is that the service must all be related to the
idea of death. Hence it is hard to avoid monotony. While
there are certain to be readings and prayers, and there may
be additional elements, all of them have to do with one
grim subject. The tone color throughout is likely to be somber, if not doleful. Even if the service lasts only twenty
minutes, the time may seem long. There are few contrasting
hues, with lights and shades. There may be no alternating
currents of thought and feeling. In short, there may be
need of a better plan.

A kindred difficulty is that there may be only one leading

voice. If there were singing by the congregation, or the repetition of The Lord's Prayer and the Apostles' Creed in unison, there would be a measure of corporate worship. But ordinarily the pastor must be the spokesman for both God and people. In no other kind of worship, except a sermon, does the minister speak for twenty or thirty minutes uninterruptedly. In the Sunday message there is more variety of spirit and substance than in many a funeral service. Partly for this reason, such exercises may seem long.

If the services were like a land of hills and valleys, the effect would be cumulative. But there is difficulty in providing for two or three climactic stages. Instead of having everything on a dead level, there should be two or three places where the thought and feeling culminate. At any such climactic stage the wise thing to do is to pause for a moment, and then proceed, perhaps with a lower tone of voice. Without seeming hurried or jerky, the movement should be progressive. Variety is restful. If it is lacking, the basic plan may call for revision.

The chief difficulty is not in devising the program but in using it as a means of comfort and not as an end in itself. Instead of thinking further about the theory, therefore, let us glance at a homemade ritual. It scarcely deserves such an imposing title, for the chief mark of it all is simplicity. In a service lasting little more than twenty minutes, and intended to reach the heart rather than the head, anything except simplicity would seem out of place.

Sometimes the list is shorter than the one below. It is easier to omit than to add. But if there is singing, the list needs to be longer. With three musical selections, have one at the beginning and one after each prayer; with two, omit the first; with one, have it after either of the prayers.

The Call to Worship

One or Two Short Psalms

A Brief Prayer—Adoration and Confession

The New Testament Readings

Brief Remarks (Omit?)

A Brief Poem (Omit?)

The Pastoral Prayer

The Lord's Prayer

The Priestly Benediction

THE PRACTICAL WORKINGS

Let us watch the plan at work. The call to worship should be deliberate. The tone should be low in pitch, but with no little volume. Strive as a man will to keep his voice down, it tends to rise. The effect is more pleasing if he starts with a tone that is low but clearly audible. In reading the two short psalms, or else a longer one, the rate of speech depends on the spirit of the words. The Ninetieth Psalm, for instance, requires more deliberate utterance than the Ninety-first. As a rule the latter is more in keeping with the uplift of a Christian service.

The first part of the worship may reach its climax at the end of the brief prayer, which ought to require less than a minute. After a brief pause come the New Testament readings. Here too the impression should be that of deliberateness and dignity. While clearly audible, the voice need not be loud. It should never seem boisterous, but it should be masculine and authoritative. The readings from the New Testament are the most vital portion of the service. If the passages are arranged in due order, they lead up to another climax. A certain minister always closes with a part of the fourteenth chapter of John; another, with a passage from the Apocalypse.

If there are remarks they should be short. There is time to bring out only one luminous idea. It should appeal to the heart. Much more important is the pastoral prayer. It should lead up to The Lord's Prayer, which comes at this stage more fittingly than near the beginning of the service. According to the plan before us, this is the only part of the main service in which everyone present takes part. The fact that The Lord's Prayer is dear to every heart makes it all the more fitting here. In a funeral it is often the old rather than the new that brings people close to God. After The Lord's Prayer they should receive the benediction.

For services in the sanctuary, or elsewhere with music, there may be need of a longer list. Still the basic pattern is much the same. It calls for alternate emphasis on speaking to God for the people, and then addressing the people in the name of God. If there is singing by the people, however, they can speak for themselves. Likewise there is a wholesome sense of corporate worship when they join in repeating the Apostles' Creed and The Lord's Prayer. Thus the exercises need not be merely a ministerial monologue.

Whatever the order, the value of the service depends far more on the spirit of the leader and on his selection of materials than on the sequence of the parts. In fact, one could follow an ideal order in a wooden way, just as one might have a helpful service without much semblance of a pattern. But since there are sure to be many funerals in the course of a man's ministry, he will save time and energy if early in his career he determines how he will conduct a service of farewell. In any one case, however, he may have to vary his plans so as to meet human needs.

Thus it appears that a minister who follows a ritual of his own devising ought to be something of a poet as well as a seer. The spirit of worship is closely akin to the beauty of verse. When love for God and his sorrowing people fills the heart of the minister as he makes his plans, and then carries them out, materials that in other hands might seem wooden become vital and moving. At times there may be a touch of splendor. From this point of view look at the following plan for a funeral in the sanctuary. The time is summer, early in the afternoon.

Organ Music—Familiar Hymn Tunes

Hymn by the People: "Our God, Our Help in Ages
Past" . . . . *Croft*

The Reading of Psalm 91

The Prayer of Adoration and Confession

Hymn by the People: "Beneath the Cross of Jesus" . *Maker*

The Apostles' Creed

The Readings from the New Testament

The Obituary (Omit?)

The Pastor's Message (Omit?)

Special Vocal Music: "God So Loved the World" . *Stainer*

The Pastoral Prayer

The Lord's Prayer

The Priestly Benediction

Organ Music: "Jerusalem the Golden" . . . . *Ewing*

THE LOOSE-LEAF NOTEBOOK

For use at funerals and elsewhere, the minister should have a loose-leaf notebook. It ought to be small enough to fit snugly in a side pocket, and large enough to hold leaves or cards four by six inches. In the portion set aside for funerals there should be room for any brief prayer that he wishes to read, as well as Scripture lessons, poems, and other materials. As a rule there is need of no other book, either during the main services or at the cemetery. If he always writes out such materials, he will keep them from being long.

When the materials are not in use they can repose in the files. The heading may be "Funerals." There may well be separate listings for each kind of material, so that the readings suitable for a child's funeral will not become confused with those for an aged saint. When the call comes to make ready for an unexpected service, the minister can turn to his files, take out what he wishes to use, and then arrange the parts according to his purpose. On his return from the cemetery he can replace all the materials in the files. If he wishes to note where he has used any item, such information belongs on the reverse side of the card.

The description makes the matter seem mechanical. But really it is only a common sense way of conserving time when every moment is precious. However, this way of working is not so simple as it seems. No worthy plan operates automatically. In some circumstances it may require most of the morning to prepare for a funeral that will last only twenty minutes. In any case it is a source of satisfaction to have at hand, available instantly, the fruitage of past reading and thinking. It is also convenient to have the notebook ready to receive the materials as they come out of the treasure chest.

Such a method would not be safe in the hands of a literalist or a worldling. But if the minister has a heart as well as a head, and if he employs both for the glory of God, in order to comfort his children, the use of a basic plan, with fresh materials each time, will enable him to find in this part of his work enduring satisfactions. Nevertheless, he must ever be on his guard lest he substitute a working method for a living faith.

VII. The Available Music

NOWHERE in the funeral service is there more need of a reform than in the music. In some circles the tendency has been to sweep away everything of the sort. But when those who mourn express a desire for hymns or other music, the request is reasonable. Did not the Protestant Reformation encourage God's people to sing? If the selections are wisely made and properly rendered, even by amateurs, music has power to bind up the broken in heart.

The right sort of music goes far to insure variety and spiritual helpfulness. Like the flowers that some of the fathers used to ban from the funeral service, music affords the children of God "beauty for ashes, the oil of joy for mourning, the garment of praise for the spirit of heaviness" (Isa. 61: 3).

There need not be music at every funeral. In the writer's experience there has often been none. But it so happens that there has been something of the kind in almost every funeral that he recalls with satisfaction. This may be due to the fact that he is a lover of music, especially hymns. So are many others who attend funeral services.

In arranging for such services the author made it a rule to ask whether or not the friends desired music. He was careful not to express an opinion one way or the other. Except in summer, when funerals were few, he was asked for music two or three times a month. If the people wished for the presence of expert musicians, who received compensation on the Lord's Day, he explained the situation, and had nothing to do with securing their services. But if volunteer singers were acceptable, he offered to provide them, without cost.

In every congregation of any size there are godly women who are glad to sing at funerals. In each of his parishes the writer found at least two volunteer singers, either of whom could play the tunes on the piano. If one of them could not be present on a certain afternoon, she was able to send a substitute. These volunteers seldom ventured to sing anything but hymns. That was what the members of the family desired. Those who wish music at funerals are old-fashioned folk, who love hymns about Christ and the Cross.

THE LIMITED RANGE

In such circumstances the range is likely to be limited. The people usually ask for the old stand-bys. If so, the minister accedes to the desires of the family. Without seeming facetious, one might say that the minister should remember that this is to be "their funeral." But if at heart he is a home missionary of music he can promote the cause at certain funerals. While the hymns that are usually asked for include some of the noblest in the English tongue, there is need of a wider range.

When the services are held in the sanctuary the singing may be by the people. With a capable organist and someone to lead the congregation there can be effective choral music, with no special numbers. Consequently there may be a sort of variety out of the question when the minister alone takes part from beginning to end. There is also the feeling of restfulness and uplift resulting from the right sort of Christian songs. There may even be exultation.

It was so one afternoon in Miller Chapel at Princeton Seminary. At the services in memory of former President Stevenson the sanctuary was thronged. No one was dressed in mourning. There were three hymns, each sung by the congregation, and there was no other music save that of the organ as the people entered and as they departed from the sanctuary. The list below is due to the loving-kindness of the one who chose the songs as expressions of her husband's devotion to Christ and the Church:

"The King of Love My Shepherd Is."
"O Saviour, Precious Saviour."
"Ten Thousand Times Ten Thousand."

At the funeral of President Stevenson's brother-in-law, Professor J. Y. Simpson, of Edinburgh University, the two hymns were chosen in much the same manner and for exactly the same purpose. They were: "Be Still, My Soul: the Lord Is on Thy Side" and "Ten Thousand Times Ten Thousand." A study of the first hymn will show the spirit with which the lonely believer faces the future, unafraid. When the words are sung to "Finlandia" the appeal is all the more plaintive. Toward the end of the service the second hymn would be glorious by contrast. Together the two come close to the heart of the Christian faith.

As a rule our funeral music is melancholy. It need not be so. Within the same family circle as above, farewell services were held at Indianapolis in memory of the aged father. For years he had served as a leading Christian layman. At last a host of his friends came together in the sanctuary to celebrate his home-going. The concluding song was the "Hallelujah Chorus" from Handel's "Messiah." Surely that is closer to the heart of our holy faith than the sort of lugubrious music that used to be common at funerals. At other services it may be wholesome to stress the somber side of our mortal existence, but at the home-going of an aged saint the call is for peans of triumph. "For all the saints who from their labors rest, . . . Alleluia!"

Whoever selects the hymns ought to know music as well as poetry. While there is room for pleasing variety, each song ought to be the best of its kind. By the best, one refers only to what is available and feasible. The range may be limited to the hymns in the church hymnal. The choice there is restricted to those that the available musicians can render for the glory of God. Not many amateurs can play or sing acceptably the creations of Beethoven and Bach. Obviously, the more limited the ability of the musicians is, the more care will be necessary in making the selections.

If the pastor does not know how to choose hymns, he can secure help from his wife, or someone else who is at home in realms of beauty. Gradually he can learn how to select songs that will voice the various moods appropriate at a funeral service. From his treasury the pastor can bring forth songs old and new. As a rule the old will predominate. Many of the people, especially among the aged, prefer the old favorites. In time he will learn how to keep the balance between the old songs and the new. Gradually he can increase the range.

THE OLD HYMNS

By the old hymns one means those that are common at funerals. In this respect local customs vary. In the writer's experience the repertoire has been much as follows: "Abide with Me"; "Asleep in Jesus"; "He Leadeth Me"; "In the Cross of Christ I Glory"; "Jesus, Lover of My Soul"; "Jesus, Saviour, Pilot Me"; "My Faith Looks Up to Thee"; "Nearer, My God, to Thee"; "Peace, Perfect Peace"; "Rock of Ages"; "The Old Rugged Cross"; "There Is a Land of Pure Delight"; "What a Friend We Have in Jesus"; and "When Peace, Like a River."

To most of these songs there can be little objection. Doctrinally, nearly all are in line with the teachings of the New Testament. Without some of them at hand, the pastor might often feel at a loss. Putting them together, however, one feels that something more is needful. Speaking broadly, one finds too much about "death's cold, sullen stream," and too little about the joys of the New Jerusalem. With certain exceptions, the music is neither restful nor uplifting.

In funeral services there should be a place for songs like

those listed above. But the range should be wider. In the additional hymns there should be more stress on what is dominant in the New Testament, as it deals with the last great enemy, death. Instead of attempting to define the difference, let us look at the lists below. No one of the three groups is better, perhaps, than the list above. But by making selections from the old favorites and these other groups one can secure wholesome variety.

If anyone wishes to sense the difference, let him spend an evening with his wife at the piano. Together let them sing a stanza or two of each hymn listed above, and then do the same with the songs that appear below. In each case the list is suggestive, rather than exhaustive. It merely shows some of the possibilities. With the help of the church organist and the leader of the choir, the pastor and his wife can make lists more suitable for the home parish.

The songs listed below are in the standard hymnals of the various Churches. The order of arrangement is alphabetical. The first list includes hymns that may come early in the funeral service. The second group consists of those that may be more fitting in the heart of the worship. The third section comprises those that may be suitable just before the benediction. But these groupings are subject to various modifications.

When a funeral service calls for three hymns, each should be somewhat different from the other two. The choice and the arrangement depend on the basic pattern of the service. If in his spare time the pastor makes up lists of hymns appropriate at the beginning, the middle, and the end of such a service as he often conducts, he will have in his files a treasure store on which he can draw in the hour of need.

The compiling of the lists will deepen the minister's love for the hymnbook. Apart from the Bible, the church book of praise is the most precious thing in any man's study. Through the hymnal the pastor will come close to the God who loves to reveal Himself in the beauty of holiness.

"Angel voices, ever singing" [for a child]
"Brightly gleams our banner" [for a child]
"Come, thou almighty King"
"Come, thou Fount of every blessing"
"Come, ye disconsolate, where'er ye languish"
"Come, ye thankful people, come"
"Gloria in Excelsis" (Old Scottish chant)
"Hark! hark, my soul! angelic songs are swelling" (evening)
"Now the day is over" (evening)
"Now thank we all our God"
"Our God, our Help in ages past"
"Unto the hills around do I lift up" ("Sandon")
"Upward where the stars are burning"

✿ ✿ ✿ ✿

"Beneath the cross of Jesus"
"Brief life is here our portion"
"Come, O thou Traveler unknown"
"How firm a foundation, ye saints of the Lord"
"I heard the voice of Jesus say"
"I'm but a stranger here"
"Love divine, all loves excelling"
"My God, my Father, while I stray" (a chant)
"O God of Bethel, by whose hand"
"O Love that wilt not let me go" ✓
"O sacred Head, now wounded" (tune difficult)
"Saviour, like a Shepherd lead us" [for a child]
"The King of love my Shepherd is"
"The Lord's my Shepherd, I'll not want"
"There is a green hill far away"
"When I survey the wondrous cross" ("Hamburg")

✿ ✿ ✿ ✿

"Around the throne of God in heaven" [for a child]
"Crown Him with many crowns"
"For all the saints who from their labors rest"
"Guide me, O thou great Jehovah"
"I heard a sound of voices"
"Jerusalem the golden"

"Lead, kindly Light, amid th' encircling gloom" ("Sandon")
"Now the laborer's task is o'er"
"One sweetly solemn thought"
"O Jesus, I have promised"
"O mother dear, Jerusalem"
"O what their joy and their glory must be" (O Quanta Qualia)
"Sunset and evening star"
"Ten thousand times ten thousand"

THE ORGAN MUSIC

A funeral service in the sanctuary calls for music from the organ. If the friends wish for silence, save when the minister is speaking, they should have their way. But few will object to soft, meditative harmonies as the people come into the House of Prayer, and something more uplifting as they go out toward the cemetery. Like the beauty of the flowers and the stained glass windows, the right sort of music from the organ tends to foster the spirit of Christian peace and hope.

Sometimes there need be nothing more than the melodies of standard hymns. The appeal of music is to the heart. The spiritual value comes chiefly through association. Hence there should be a blessing when the organist plays tunes like those in the list below. At any one service the choice of the tunes depends on various factors. For instance, the melodies played while the people are assembling should be more meditative than the music while the throng is leaving the sanctuary. With such a setting of beauty there is abundance of room for lights and shadows. As a rule the lights should prevail.

The list that follows is suggestive, not exhaustive. It does not include the tunes of the "old" funeral hymns: Adeste Fideles, Alford, Aurelia, Austrian Hymn, Beecher, Bentley, Diademata, Dundee, Evening Praise, Eventide (Monk), Finlandia, Hamburg, In Babilone, Love Divine (Le Jeune), Morecambe, Old 124th, O Quanta Qualia, Palestrina, Passion Chorale, Pilgrims (Smart), Portuguese Hymn, Saint Anne,

Sandon, Schönster Herr Jesu, Sine Nomine (R. V. Williams), and Vox Dilecti.

For simple music from the organ the pastor may rely on a volunteer who loves to play for the glory of God. When the regular organist is present there may be special music that is more difficult. In either case the idea is to afford the service a background of quiet beauty. Otherwise the atmosphere of a church partly filled may seem cold and desolate. At a funeral parlor, also, the right sort of instrumental music tends to soften hearts and prepare them to receive the ministry of words.

When a volunteer plays hymn tunes on the organ she will be glad if the pastor makes the selections. But when there is to be special music the organist wishes to decide what she shall play. However, she will appreciate from the minister a statement of what he has in view. As a lover of beauty she knows that the tone color of the organ music ought to be in harmony with the spirit of the hour. Hitherto she may have ministered with clergymen whose conduct of the services called for a funeral march by Chopin or Grieg. She will be relieved to learn that it is proper to render selections pitched in a major key.

Among melodies suitable for funerals there is endless variety. However, there are certain restrictions. Each number should be restful or uplifting. The associations ought to be Christian. For aid in compiling the list below the author is indebted to friends at the Westminster Choir College, notably Alexander McCurdy, D. Mus.; Mrs. Harry Krimmel; James Weeks; and Philip T. Blackwood. For the final selections, however, the writer alone is responsible. Among the various proposals he has retained numbers that are likely to be available for the organist of the average church.

Bach, J. S. . . . . . "Hark! a Voice Saith, All Is Mortal"
  "O God, Have Mercy"
  "Our Father, Thou Art in Heaven Above"
  "Our Father, Who Art in Heaven"

Brahms	"Deck Thyself, My Soul"
	"A Lovely Rose Is Blooming"
	"O Sacred Head Now Wounded"
	"O World, I Now Must Leave Thee"
Dupré	"Cortège et Litanie"
	"He, Remembering His Great Mercy"
Franck, César	Andante from "Grande Pièce Symphonique"
Greenfield	"Prelude in Olden Style"
Guilmant, A.	"Funeral March and Song of the Seraphs"
	"Prayer and Cradle Song"
Karg-Elert	"Adorn Thyself, O My Soul"
	"O God, Thou Faithful God"
	"Rejoice Greatly, O My Soul"
Mendelssohn, F.	Adagio from "The First Organ Sonata"
Muffat, G.	Adagio from "Toccata"
Purvis	"Communion"

THE SPECIAL SONGS

The special vocal music is likely to cause more concern than all the hymns and organ numbers combined. If the members of the family secure the singer, the resulting solo may be "Beautiful Isle of Somewhere," or another number equally non-Christian. When sweetly rendered by a gifted soprano such a song may be pleasing, but there may be in it scarcely a word or a suggestion that would be out of place in a Hebrew synagogue or a gathering of secular humanists. Quartet numbers may be equally lacking in Christian content and spirit.

In the course of time many of these conditions will right themselves. Sensitiveness to what is proper in worship seems to be growing. Other branches of the Church are beginning to follow the Protestant Episcopal practice of forbidding in the sanctuary vocal music that is non-Biblical. At marriages the Roman Church has recently issued a ban against such songs as "Oh Promise Me." The same principle, when applied to funerals, will go far to remedy the present musical secularism. As a rule it is wise to bring about reforms gradually, with no blaring of trumpets.

The way to promote the use of worthy special music at funerals is to guide in the choice of such numbers as those that appear below. In compiling the list the author is indebted to the friends named above. The majority of the following selections are only moderately difficult. Nevertheless, they ought to be attempted only by persons who can sing correctly and with skill. Unless real musicians are available, it is much better to have simple hymns than to suffer while well-meaning members of an "awkward squad" are doing their utmost to "rend the anthem."

In time it should also be possible to use chants. Especially do the psalms lend themselves to this kind of uplifting worship. After the singers have learned how to chant, and the people have become accustomed to this way of ascribing glory to God, nothing will add more distinction to the funeral service than to have the chanting of such a psalm as the Fifteenth, Twenty-third, Twenty-fourth, Twenty-seventh, Thirty-ninth, Forty-sixth, Ninetieth, Ninety-first, One Hundred and Third, or One Hundred and Twenty-first.

ANTHEMS

Bach, J. S.	"Now Let Every Tongue Adore Thee"
	"Ah, How Fleeting"
Barnby, J.	"Crossing the Bar"
Barnby-Lewis . . .	"Now the Day Is Over" (men's voices)
Chadwick, G. W. .	"When Our Heads Are Bowed with Woe"
Gaul, A. R. . . .	"Great and Marvelous" ("The Holy City")
	"No Shadows Yonder" ("The Holy City")
Gounod, C. . . .	"Forever with the Lord" (quartet)
	"Unfold, Ye Portals Everlasting" ("Redemption")
Grieg, E.	"Jesu, Friend of Sinners"
Haydn, F. J. . . .	"Lo, My Shepherd Is Divine"
Matthews, J. S. . .	"I Heard a Voice from Heaven"

Mendelssohn, F. . . . "Forever Blest Are They" (men's voices)
                       "Happy and Blest Are They"
                       "He That Shall Endure to the End"
Noble, T. Tertius .   "The Souls of the Righteous"
Parker, H. W. . . .   "The Lord Is My Light"
Spohr, L. . . . .   "Blest Are the Departed"
Shelley, H. R. . . .   "Crossing the Bar" (solo, low voice, with
                          chorus)
Stainer, J. . . . .   "God So Loved the World"
                       "My Hope Is in the Everlasting"
Tschaikowsky-Cain .   "O Blest Are They"

SOLOS AND DUETS

Christiansen, F. M. "I Know a Home Eternal" (baritone)
Franck, César . . . "O Lord Most Holy"
Gaul, A. R. . . .   "They Shall Hunger No More" (soprano
                        and alto)
Gounod, C. . . .   "Forever with the Lord" (duet, high and
                        low)
Handel, G. F.   "Come Unto Him" (soprano)
                     "He Shall Feed His Flock" (alto)
                     "I Know That My Redeemer Liveth"
                        (All from "The Messiah")

Handel-Milligan   . "Immortal Love" (high)
Kingsley, R. . . .   "Immortality"
MacDermid, J. G. .   "In My Father's House"
Shelley, H. R. . . . "Hark, Hark, My Soul"
Ward-Stephens . .   "In My Father's House"
Willeby, C. . . . . "Crossing the Bar" (duet, high and low)

Informational Readings

Breed, David Riddle, *History and Use of Hymns and Hymn-tunes*.
    Fleming H. Revell Company, 1934.
Gilbert, Harry, Editor, *Gilbert's Manual for Choir-Loft and Pulpit*.
    Charles Scribner's Sons, 1939.
Hjortsvang, Carl, *The Amateur Choir Director*. Abingdon-Cokesbury
    Press, 1941.
Randall, Mallinson, Editor, *The Choirmaster's Guide to the Selection
    of Hymns and Anthems*. H. W. Gray Company, 1911.

VIII. The Scripture Readings

THE simplest way to better the average funeral service would be to improve the selection of the Scripture readings. Sometimes there is music; often there is not. But there is always at least one passage from the Bible. Usually there are several. If there is no sermon, the readings from the Book afford the only opportunity to throw light from above on the mystery of death. If the pastor chooses aright, and reads with distinction, portions of Holy Writ will reach and bless many a heart. What could be more vital?

But, alas, the selections are often unwise. Instead of choosing passages that throw light on present needs, a man may pick up a book of forms and without preparation stumble through a succession of passages that have little continuity, no climax, and no power to soothe. In one of the older books there are on two small pages fifteen varied passages, from nine books of the Bible. Even if the reader were well prepared, how could he secure any harmony of tone color?

In the older books of forms the funeral readings were often melancholy. In the New Testament after the resurrection of our Lord there is from the lips of a believer scarcely a note of pessimism. But in some of our funeral services most of the Scripture passages are gloomy, not to say despairing. "Man that is born of woman hath but a short time to live, and is full of misery." "He heapeth up riches, and knoweth not who shall gather them." "Vanity of vanities, saith the Preacher, all is vanity and vexation of spirit."

All of that is true, and it ought to be told. But there are other occasions when one can speak about "the dark line in God's face." When the sun is shining and the south wind is blowing softly, there may be need of warning the mariner that the winter is drawing nigh. But when the tempest has broken forth in fury and all seems likely to be lost, there is a call for words of sympathy and hope. Especially if the deceased has been a radiant Christian, the emphasis at his funeral should be on the glory of our holy faith.

In recent years the books of forms have been largely free from such faults. They have put in the forefront psalms like the Twenty-third and the One Hundred and Third. The other selections are mainly from the New Testament. As a rule each passage is a unit. While it may not be long, there is completeness of thought and feeling. There is little of the old "hop, skip, and jump" reading that used to make the Scriptures seem disjointed. Consequently, if a clergyman is in doubt concerning what to read at a funeral service he can fall back on his favorite book of forms.

SELECTING THE PASSAGES

Ordinarily the minister wishes to select passages inspired of God to meet the sort of needs that will face him in the approaching funeral. In the Scriptures not only does he look for certain strains of thought and feeling; he likewise notes the tone color. Even within any one book each literary unit is likely to have a tone color all its own. By careful choice of materials he can produce harmony of effect, and increasing warmth of spirit, as the succession of beautiful words leads the hearers closer and closer to God.

The first reading is usually from The Book of Psalms. If each of them is short, there may be two. But if the selection is the Ninety-first, or the One Hundred and Third, a single psalm is enough. At an occasional funeral, where the departed is aged, the Ninetieth Psalm may be in order. But as a rule the Ninety-first is more in keeping with the spirit of the hour. At other times the minister should stress the solemn truths voiced by the Ninetieth Psalm. But when those whom he loves are sitting under the shadow of death they need to lift up their hearts as in one of the more radiant songs.

As a rule there need be no other selection from the Old Testament. But if it seems wise to have a passage from any other part of the Old Testament, this comes as the first of what we designate as "New Testament Readings." For instance, at the funeral of a practical woman whose name was Martha, the pastor read ten or twelve verses from the closing chapter of Proverbs. In that prose poem there are twenty-two verses, but only ten or twelve may be of special interest at a funeral today. By careful selection of verses one can secure continuity and likewise preserve the tone color.

After a slight pause, and with a change of tone, the minister read from the Gospels about the way the Lord Jesus loved Martha, as well as Mary. Then came another brief pause, with a shift of tone, after which he read a passage from the Epistles and one from the Apocalypse. The entire service, including the Ninety-first Psalm at the beginning, called for five readings, no one of which was long.

As a rule it is wise to have only a few separate passages. Five or six is a good upper limit. If the number were higher there would probably be a scattering of interest. Even when the total number is not large, each passage ought to be fairly short. In dealing with the fifteenth chapter of First Corinthians, for example, one scarcely knows what to do. To read it aloud as a whole would require perhaps seven minutes. Even if one started with verse 20, the remainder of the chapter might seem heavy. In the lists that appear below, this golden chapter is broken into a number of passages, each of which seems to form a complete unit.

The same principle of feeling free to select certain parts applies to other chapters, such as the fortieth chapter of Isaiah or the fourth chapter of Philippians. In the latter passage the writer would begin with verse 4, read through verse 8, and then pass on to verse 13, finishing with verse 19. By this means he would have in seven verses the heart of all that the apostle here tells about Christian contentment. At a funeral there is seldom any announcement of what passage one is reading; hence there need be no reference to the omissions.

As a rule the best version for use at a funeral is the King James Version. While it has minor flaws, the language is notable for beauty. Even the prose has a pleasing rhythm. The diction has a dignity and elevation rarely found in recent translations. The fact that the old version is familiar makes it welcome in the time of sorrow. That is when the heart cries out for the old faith and the familiar landmarks, as they appear in mother's Bible.

A case will show how the principle works. At services held in memory of an aged friend the minister read a few of her favorite psalms. That was the kind thing to do, as she had been a lifelong singer of the psalms. The list had been prepared by her daughters, who singled out the Twenty-third as the psalm that their mother had loved most. But to their dismay the minister began the reading with the words, "Jehovah is my Shepherd." At such a time a little thing may loom large. To her dying day each of those daughters will think of that reading as the only unfortunate feature of their mother's coronation service.

Without being spectacular or bizarre, such readings ought to be memorable. They should appeal to the heart and likewise kindle the imagination. They should suggest something for the eye to see, for the heart to feel, and for the will to do. Erelong the sorrowing friends should go out feeling that they have been with the Lord Jesus on the mountaintop and that they will walk with him on earth until their traveling days are done.

PREPARING TO READ

Whenever there is time to make ready for a funeral, a good deal of thought should go into the study of the Scripture readings. One way to prepare would be to learn them by heart and then recite them without glancing at the printed

page. Every minister should commit to memory golden portions of the Book, the more the better. But as a rule the pastoi
who best knows the Book prefers to read the Scriptures. One
reason is that the interpreter should call attention to the
Bible, not to himself. Occasionally, however, one hears a
clergyman who can recite the Scriptures without an air of
showmanship. Down in his heart every minister should determine that he will read so as to exalt the Saviour and not
the self.

Whatever the method, the pastor should be prepared. He
ought to understand each passage. Without pausing for
comment, he should be able to interpret the revealed will
of God. Hence he should know which words to stress, and
when to pause, as well as how long. Otherwise the emphasis
might fall on the wrong word. Instead of singling out the
verb and the noun, the reader might thump the preposition
and the pronoun. Instead of stressing a single word in a
clause, he might attempt to make every syllable stand out.
Instead of bringing out the prose rhythm of the old King
James, he might resort to a singsong swing.

One difficulty about interpreting the Bible is that each passage calls for a different treatment. How else could the minister bring out the tone color? Such excellence in reading is
rare. It comes through living with the words until the soul
is in accord with their mystic harmonies. When a wise interpreter comes to the funeral service he makes everyone feel
that the Lord is the Good Shepherd, here and now; and that
in the Father's home there are many rooms for the redeemed
children of God. With a few passages interpreted by one who
can read, there may be no call for a sermon.

A good way to prepare in general is to make a loving study
of each passage that is likely to be needed at a funeral. The
man who dwells at "the house of the Interpreter" spends a
good deal of time each day in mastering some part of the
Book. When the study of any passage is complete, the words

themselves may be written on a separate card or a loose-leaf sheet, all ready for his files. If there is a secretary, she can do this work; but if the minister does it himself, he will love the words all the more. How could he spend his spare time more profitably than in working over luminous passages about the life everlasting?

When there is a call for a funeral, with little time to make ready, the interpreter can quickly select from his files a few passages inspired to meet the present needs. Then he can read them, one by one, so as to bring the hearers close to the heart of God. Even in a service that lasts only twenty minutes, he can guide his sorrowing friends into the mountaintop. There they will behold the Lord Jesus and begin to be transformed into his likeness.

Such is the theory. The lists following show how the plan works. In time a minister ought to have ready for use passages of various kinds. The arrangement here is Biblical rather than topical. It matters little how a man stores his treasures, provided he can quickly lay his hand on what he wishes to use. The writer has found it best to file such material according to the book, the chapter, and the verse in the Bible. However, he is vastly more concerned with the meaning and the use of the Scriptures than with any method of classification.

Psalm 1.	The Blessedness of Being Good.
Psalm 15.	The Portrait of a Godly Man.
Psalm 16.	The Song of the Saint.
Psalm 23.	The Goodness of the Shepherd.
Psalm 24.	The Glory of Our King (use at the grave?).
Psalm 27.	The Psalm of the Soldier.
Ps. 34: 1-19.	The Goodness of Our God.
Psalm 39.	The Gloom of the Grave (use seldom).
Ps. 42: 1-5.	The Shadow in the Soul.
Psalm 46.	The God of the Battlefield.

Psalm 90.	The Shadow of Eternity (for an aged person).
Psalm 91.	The Security of the Saint.
Psalm 103.	The Loving-Kindness of the Father.
Psalm 116.	The Sorrows of the Saint.
Ps. 119: 9-16.	The Religion of a Young Man.
Psalm 121.	The Song of the Pilgrim (use at the grave?).
Psalm 130.	The Prayer of the Desolate.
Psalm 139.	The Cry of the Lonely Soul (use only a part).

❧ ❧ ❧ ❧

Gen., ch. 50.	The Burial of a Godly Father.
Ruth 1: 16-22.	The Loyalty of the Loving Heart.
II Sam. 12: 16-23.	The Home-Going of a Baby.
Job 14: 1-14.	The Hope of Immortality.
Job 19: 23-27.	The Assurance of the Resurrection.
Prov. 31: 10-31.	The Portrait of a Godly Woman.
Eccl. 12: 1-7, 13, 14.	The Dissolution of the Body.
Isa. 40: 1-11, 28-31.	The Message of God's Comfort.
Isa. 43: 1-3a.	The Power of God to Redeem.
Isa. 63: 7-9.	The Grace of God for the Sorrowful.

❧ ❧ ❧ ❧

Matt. 5: 1-16.	The Blessedness of God's Children.
Matt. 6: 19-34.	The Security of Heavenly Treasures.
Matt. 7: 18-27.	The Christian Secret of Security.
Matt. 11: 25-30.	The Master's Gift of Rest.
Matt. 18: 1-6.	The Saviour with the Child.
Matt. 18: 10-14.	The Shepherd with His Lambs.
Matt. 25: 1-13.	The Meaning of Religion as Readiness.
Matt. 25: 31-40.	The Surprises of the Judgment Day.
Mark 5: 22, 23, 35-43.	The Death of a Growing Girl (aged 12).
Mark 10: 13-16.	The Lord's Blessing on Little Children.

Luke 7: 11-15.	The Death of an Only Son.
Luke 10: 38-42.	The Joys of Being with Jesus.
Luke 23: 33-47.	The Love of the Dying Saviour.
Luke 24: 13-35.	The Fellowship of the Risen Lord.
John 10: 7-16.	The Goodness of Our Shepherd.
John 11: 11-26.	The Promise of the Resurrection.
John 14: 1-18, 25-28.	The Meaning of Heaven as Home.
John 15: 1-17.	The Christian Secret of Fruitfulness.
Rom. 8: 18-28.	The Wonders of God's Providence.
Rom. 8: 31-39.	The Power of God over Death.
I Cor., ch. 13.	The Supremacy of Christian Love.
I Cor. 15: 20-28.	The Beginning of the Eternal Harvest.
I Cor. 15: 35-49.	The Glory of the Heavenly Harvest.
I Cor. 15: 50-58.	The Power of Christ over the Grave.
II Cor. 4: 5-18.	The Power of God in Man's Weakness.
II Cor. 5: 1-10.	The Hope of Going Home.
Eph. 6: 10-18.	The Completeness of the Christian Armor.
Phil. 2: 5-11.	The Glory of the Incarnate Lord.
Phil. 3: 7-16.	The Power of Christ's Resurrection.
Phil. 4: 4-9, 13, 19.	The Christian Secret of Contentment.
I Thess. 4: 13-18.	The Promise of the Second Coming.
I Thess. 5: 1-11, 23, 24.	The Comfort of the Christian Hope.
Titus 2: 11-14.	The Gospel of Christian Hope.
Heb. 11: 1-10.	The Title Deeds of Heaven.
Heb. 11: 32 to 12: 2.	The Faith of Our Fathers.
Heb. 12: 1-14.	The Meaning of God's Chastening.
I Peter 1: 1-9.	The Glory of the Christian Hope.
I Peter 2: 11, 12, 19-25.	The Beauty of Christian Suffering.
I John 1: 1-9.	The Glory of God as Light.
I John 2: 12-17.	The Religion of the Family.
I John 3: 16-24.	The Meaning of Religion as Love.
I John 4: 7-21.	The Victory of Love over Fear.
Rev. 7: 9-17.	The Joys of the Heavenly Host.
Rev. 21: 1-7.	The Glory of the Heavenly City.
Rev. 21: 22-27.	The Lights of the Eternal City.
Rev. 22: 1-7.	The River of Life Everlasting.

Informational Readings

Blackwood, Andrew W., *The Fine Art of Public Worship*. The Cokesbury Press, 1939. Chapter VII.

Curry, Samuel Silas, *Vocal and Literary Interpretation of the Bible*. Doubleday, Doran & Co., 1910.

IX. The Pastor's Prayers

THE most difficult part of the funeral service is the prayers. Except for the Scripture lessons, nothing else begins to be so vital. In fact, the minister often dispenses with everything except the readings and the prayers. In a Christian service this is usually the minimum. There may be nothing more, but there should always be a word from the heart of God, as well as a prayer addressed to him. In all Christian worship, and not least at a funeral, these two belong together. Either without the other would be incomplete.

In the plan for the service each prayer may follow a reading from the Bible. If so, the principle is that of alternating. In the readings the minister is speaking for God to the hearts of his children. In the prayers the pastor is addressing the heavenly Father on behalf of his sons and daughters. While it is not easy to interpret the Scriptures so as to bring out the tone color, and thus use them in meeting the needs of human souls, it is even more difficult to voice the desires that should fill the hearts bowed down in grief.

In a funeral service there may be five acts of prayer. This number includes what is done at the home, or in the church, as well as at the grave. The list also includes the two benedictions. Really a benediction is not a prayer, but it belongs in the same lofty realm. If we include only a single benediction, the one at the grave, the acts of prayer in a funeral service are somewhat like those in a regular hour of morning worship.

According to the plan in mind, the first prayer comes after the reading from The Book of Psalms. The mood of the words addressed to God should be in keeping with the tone

color of what has just gone before. The minister voices the
feelings of adoration and awe that should fill the hearts
of God's children as they come into his presence and seek
his blessing. While these words are brief, they are difficult to
prepare. It is seldom easy to pray at the beginning of public
worship, and most of all in the presence of death.

For the opening prayer the minister often employs a
collect. If the people are not accustomed to the use of
written forms, he should close his eyes and speak out of
his heart. But if the friends are not averse to form in worship they should be ready to follow a historic prayer of the
Church. In deciding whether or not to read a collect, the
minister should ask whether or not his doing so will call
attention to how he is praying.

The number of suitable collects is large. This is one: "Eternal God, who lovest us with an everlasting love, help us
now to wait upon Thee with reverent and submissive hearts,
that as we hear the words of eternal life, we may through
the comfort of the Scriptures have hope in Jesus Christ,
and be lifted above our darkness and distress into the light
and peace of Thy presence, through Jesus Christ our Lord.
Amen."

After a brief pause there may be a few words of confession. This part of the funeral service is usually omitted.
If the minister does not refer to sin he may displease no
one save himself and God. Nevertheless, if he is striving to
voice the feelings that should fill the hearts of God's children as they bow down in the presence of death, he should
remember that the cause of human woe is sin.

This part of the service, while clear and impressive, should
be short and moving. A few words are enough: "Hear us, O
Father, as we confess our sins.' 'If we say that we have no sin,
we deceive ourselves. . . . If we confess our sins, he is faithful and just to forgive us our sins, and to cleanse us from all
unrighteousness. . . . And the blood of Jesus Christ his Son
cleanseth us from all sin' " (I John 1: 8, 9, 7).

Even with two elements, the prayer as a whole should be short, without seeming abrupt. If the minister speaks deliberately, as he should, the time may still be less than a minute. Even if the words are those of the minister, they may well be down in the notebook. Here again, he should read only if he can do so without calling attention to how he is praying. As a rule there is more of spiritual uplift in the opening prayer that is read, or else committed to memory, than when he speaks extempore. There is also a saving of time, which is precious.

The second prayer is usually somewhat longer. It may require two or three minutes. This prayer may come after the readings from the New Testament. The purpose is pastoral. In the earlier prayer the minister leads his friends into the presence of God and voices their feelings of penitence because they are not worthy to be called his children. In the pastoral prayer the aim is to express their emotions after they have heard from the New Testament the Gospel of peace and hope.

The pastoral prayer may begin with thanksgiving. If so, it should center round the goodness of God and the grace of the Lord Jesus Christ. Unlike the former prayer, which is somewhat general, this one should be more specific. Without resorting to eulogy, and with no attempt at appraisal of the deceased, the minister should thank God for all his goodness to the departed, and to the family circle. Needless to say, it is seldom necessary or wise to go much into detail.

It is difficult to give thanks at a funeral. A man is likely to say too little, or else too much. Unless this part of the service is planned with tenderness and taste, as well as sincerity and truthfulness, it is better not to be specific. If everything is to be general, why not read from a book? That is what one often does at a problem funeral. But if a man has the shepherd heart, he wishes to give somewhat specific thanks at the services in memory of a sainted friend.

After the brief words of thanksgiving there may be a

pause. In a different tone, somewhat lower, come the petitions for the members of the household and for others who share the sorrow. Without referring to anyone by name, the minister can present the heart needs of his friends. In these matters of the soul there are no rules. The man who knows how to pray for his people at other times will be able to intercede for them when they must walk through the dark valley.

After the petitions there should be another brief pause. Then there may be short, meaningful supplications for others who mourn. Often the minister omits this part of the service, if only because the time is limited. But if he excels in prayer, he can foster the spirit of sympathy with suffering hearts elsewhere. He knows that grief is likely to make his friends self-centered, and that they ought to share in the sorrows of the world.

Since this part of the service is pastoral it should lead up to The Lord's Prayer. If these familiar words come in the heart of the service, or else toward the end, they give everyone an opportunity to take part. If the minister is new in the parish the people may not understand that they are to join in the act of family devotion. At the first funeral or two, before the service begins, he may request the singers and a few other friends to join with him both in The Lord's Prayer and in the Apostles' Creed. These words may prove to be the climactic parts of the service.

The benediction that is most likely to accord with the service is the most beautiful of all. It comes from the Hebrew Bible. The fact that the words of blessing do not issue from the New Testament, with its triumphant assurance of the resurrection and the life everlasting, may suggest that the services thus far must be incomplete:

"The Lord bless thee, and keep thee: the Lord make his face shine upon thee, and be gracious unto thee: the Lord lift up his countenance upon thee, and give thee peace" (Num. 6: 24-26).

At the grave the prayer is usually brief. The dominant truth in this part of the service is the resurrection and the life everlasting. In view of such a blessed hope the minister voices the desire of each waiting person as he dedicates himself to God. Since life is never to end, and there is to be a family reunion in the Father's home, everyone at the grave should put himself anew into the hands of God.

Among the prayers in the funeral service, this one may be the most individual. At the opening of the exercises in the home or the church the pastor voices the feelings that should fill the hearts of God's people as they worship together. Even in the pastoral prayer, they should think of themselves as a group of the Father's children, who are looking to him for grace to supply all their needs. But at the grave each person, individually, should dedicate himself anew to the service of God and men.

At the grave the most suitable benediction is that of the covenant God (Heb. 13: 20, 21). Among all the Biblical benedictions, this one alone has to do with the Resurrection of Christ and the perfecting of the saints while they are still in the flesh. As with the words of blessing at the home or the church, the benediction at the grave is for the group as a whole. In the assurance of God's covenant peace the sorrowing friends should turn homeward and face the future unafraid.

If we look back now we shall see that the prayers over the body of a departed friend conform to a definite pattern. From funeral to funeral the content may differ widely, according to the circumstances. But the order of the prayers, as a rule, should be much the same. Whatever the circumstances, there are certain needs that the minister should have in mind as he makes ready to pray, and certain feelings that he should voice at every funeral.

In preparing to lead others as they worship God at such a time, it may help the young minister to remember the suggestion from Dean L. A. Weigle, of the Divinity School at

Yale. He says that in public prayer there should be five elements, and that the order should always be the same: adoration, confession, thanksgiving, supplication, and submission.
Under supplication he includes petitions for those present and
intercessions for others. By submission he means what we
have termed dedication.

As an aid to the memory, Dean Weigle suggests the homemade word "Actss." While such a mnemonic device may
seem wooden, if it leads to more carefully ordered prayers in
public worship, especially at the funeral service, everyone
should thank God. Even the most experienced pastor may
need to check up on his prayers, to see if there is either over-
lapping or overlooking.

When the minister leads in prayer at a funeral there should
be a basic plan for the service as a whole. Near the beginning,
and only once, he should voice the feelings of the friends
as they come consciously into the presence of God. Once, and
only once, he should express their sorrow for their sins. In the
longer prayer, and then only, he should give thanks for whatever the occasion warrants. Here, and here alone, he should
ask for what the sorrowing friends need most. At the grave,
and there only, he should give thanks for the fact of the
Resurrection, and then lead his sorrowing friends as one by
one they give themselves anew into the hands of the heavenly
Father.

The chief fact about any of these prayers is the purpose.
In each of them the aim is primarily to express feeling.
According to the Westminster Shorter Catechism, "Prayer is
an offering up of our desires." Whether the dominant mood
be that of adoration or confession, thanksgiving or petition,
intercession or dedication, that is what the friends should be
feeling. In psychological terms, the minister is striving to
"induce a desired response."

If the pastor is to lead, the people should be able to follow.
If they are not in a mood to pray, there is all the more
reason why the minister should "condition the desired

response." If he is really praying, and not simply repeating
words, his spirit should lead others to pray. If he knows
whither he is going, and how he expects to reach the goal,
he will not have to proceed alone. Otherwise there is likely
to be the blind leading of the blind.

At a funeral, as elsewhere in public worship, every prayer
should have a pattern. There should be a clear beginning
and a strong ending. There ought to be definite stages, clearly
marked. The prayer should move forward by paragraphs,
each of which ought to be fairly short. Throughout the prayer
as a whole the same tone color should prevail. In short, the
form of a prayer ought to be somewhat like that of a poem.
The spirit should be much like that of a psalm.

The language of prayer differs from that of preaching,
much as the words of poetry differ from the diction of prose.
In either case all that a man says ought to be clear and
easy to follow. In a prayer there should be even more of
quiet beauty than in a sermon. There should also be a sense
of motion. Whenever a man's heart is full of feeling his
words tend to flow in a pleasing rhythm. In the presence of
death the minister's prayers ought to be luminous with
spiritual beauty. They should also be radiant with Christian
hope.

There is time to mention only four of the many faults
that may mar the prayers at a funeral. One fault is excessive length. The cause may be lack of preparation. Another
fault is undue loudness, as though God were far away and
dull of hearing. A third is excessive speed. A fourth is im-
propriety. For instance, at the church funeral of a young
deacon the minister pleaded with God that the vacant place
in the home might soon be filled. Incidentally, the comely
young widow was married again in less than a year.

The gist of the matter is that the minister's culture and
his training, or his weaknesses in both, appear whenever he
leads in prayer at a funeral. In view of these facts the young
clergyman may exclaim, "How can I learn to pray at such

a time?" By way of reply there is nothing novel. The one who leads others to the mercy seat ought to be a good man, a hard student, and a diligent pastor. A holy man of God who has no time for special preparation can pray more acceptably than a worldling who knows almost everything except the grace of God. On the other hand, the man who loves the Lord resolves with King David: "Neither will I offer burnt offerings unto the Lord my God of that which doth cost me nothing" (II Sam. 24: 24).

Since prayer is sacrifice to God, any such exercise of the soul is costly. In other words, the minister may think of "prayer as a battlefield." When he is alone with God, he should pour out his soul. Of course he should pray often with his people, and for the nations, near and far. But first he should offer sacrifices for himself. That was what the Hebrew priest did before he dared to intercede for others. In short, if a man wishes to excel in public prayer, especially at a funeral, the training school is in the closet. Before a man tries to lead others, he himself should know the way to God.

Anyone who is troubled by wandering thoughts may form the habit of writing out a prayer each morning. At first the task may seem mechanical. But it need not be so. A written prayer may be as real as a love letter. The oftener a young man writes to the one he expects to wed, the more is he able to pour out his heart to the beloved whom he cannot behold. In prayer, as in a love letter, it is the spirit that counts. When a man's heart is overflowing with love his words are full of beauty.

Unfortunately, the more prayers a man composes, the worse he will write, unless he works carefully. In order to keep up a sense of the style that is worthy in prayer, the minister ought to own and use a number of liturgical masterpieces, beginning with *The Book of Common Prayer* of the Protestant Episcopal Church. He ought also to saturate his soul in the devotional classics, if only because their language is that of heaven come down to earth.

Among the devotional classics every man has his favorites. Those of the writer include Bunyan's *The Pilgrim's Progress* and *Grace Abounding to the Chief of Sinners,* Augustine's *Confessions,* Bishop Andrewes' *Manual of Private Devotions,* Richard Baxter's *Saints' Everlasting Rest,* and Austin Phelps's *The Still Hour.*

"There is a language of devotion," says J. Oswald Dykes,[1] "in which the young minister does well to steep himself. It has been the product of centuries of devout life. It is not a mosaic of Bible phraseology but it is modeled on Scripture examples and even more on its spirit and tone. It is a rare essence, distilled from the experience of all saints, fragrant with their concentrated devoutness.

"With classic expressions of its literature, which are not numerous, a man would need to be conversant who would catch the mingled dignity and simplicity, depth and sweetness, boldness and reverence, gravity and cheerfulness, warmth and chaste reserve, which befit the temper of Christian piety at its best."

Such is the spirit of the cloister. But if a minister is to pray aright at a funeral he ought also to be an indefatigable pastor. With his people in their homes, and likewise welcoming them one by one at his study, he should rely largely on prayer for the cure of human souls. If he prays often with his people when they are not in distress, he will know how to intercede for them when they stand face to face with the mystery of death.

In short, the minister who lives close to God and human beings will know how to make ready for leadership in prayer at a service of farewell. However brief the time to make ready for a funeral, he will spend most of the passing minutes in preparing to pray.

[1] From *The Christian Minister and His Duties,* p. 142. T. and T. Clark, Edinburgh, 1908.

On the next few pages are a number of funeral prayers. They show how ministers of various types lead sorrowing friends to the mercy seat. The prayers that come first are suitable for the early part of the service. The longer ones are more pastoral. The fifth page has a number of prayers that show what men do at the funeral of a child. Another page gives forms that have been used at the grave.

The purpose in showing these examples is to suggest that the reader start making a collection of his own. The most searching test of any such prayer is the spiritual quality. Does it move the heart Godward? Does it lead the worshiper to lift up his soul? Another test is quiet beauty. In making such a collection, as in assembling funeral poems, the minister should find refreshment for his soul.

The most suggestive and fruitful of the next few pages ought to be the last one. It contains doxologies and benedictions. The difference between the two is worthy of note: the doxology is addressed to God; the benediction, to the people. Each kind of holy words is especially fitting in the sickroom or the funeral service. Nowhere else, even in the Scriptures, can the leader of worship find so much of blessing in so little space as in some of the doxologies and benedictions. In order to use these words aright, the pastor himself ought to be a living benediction.

PRAYERS USED AT FUNERALS

Dearly beloved, seeing it hath pleased Almighty God to take unto Himself the soul of our *brother* departed, let us beseech Him to grant us His Holy Spirit, the Comforter, that our hearts may not be faint or be troubled, but may find in Him their refuge and strength. Let us pray.

Almighty God, whose will is sovereign and whose mercy is boundless, look upon us in our sorrow, and for the sake of Thy dear Son, who Himself was partaker of flesh and blood, enable us to listen to Thy Holy Word, that we through patience and comfort of the Scriptures may have hope; and grant us the consolations of Thy Holy Spirit, that, humbly confessing our manifold sins, we may hold fast the assurance of Thy favor and the hope of life everlasting, through Jesus Christ our Lord. Amen.

[From *The Directory for Public Worship*,
The Presbyterian Church of England.]

❧ ❧ ❧ ❧

Eternal God, our heavenly Father, who lovest us with an everlasting love, and canst turn the shadow of death into the morning: help us now to wait upon Thee with reverent and submissive hearts, that as we read the words of eternal life, we through patience and comfort of the Scriptures may have hope, and be lifted above our darkness and distress into the light and peace of Thy presence: through Jesus Christ, our Lord. Amen.

[From *The Book of Common Order*, 1928,
United Free Church of Scotland.]

❧ ❧ ❧ ❧

O God of Peace, who hast taught us that in returning and rest we shall be saved, in quietness and in confidence shall be our strength; By the power of Thy Spirit lift us, we pray Thee, to Thy presence, where we may be still and know that Thou art God; through Jesus Christ our Lord. Amen.

[From *The Book of Common Prayer*, According to the Use of the Protestant Episcopal Church.]

❧ ❧ ❧ ❧

O holy Father, whose mercies are from everlasting to everlasting, to Thee alone can Thy children flee for refuge in their afflictions, trusting in the assurance of Thy love. From the grief that burdens our spirits, from the sense of solitude and loss, from the doubt and fainting of the soul in its trouble, we turn to Thee. Strengthen our feeble faith, we implore Thee; comfort our hearts, and by the Gospel of Thy beloved Son speak peace to our souls. Grant this, O heavenly Father, for Jesus' sake. Amen.

[From *The Directory for Public Worship*,
The Presbyterian Church of England.]

❧ ❧ ❧ ❧

Father of all mercies and God of all comfort, who healest the broken in heart and bindest up their wounds, in mercy behold the sorrows of Thy children. Leave them not without comfort, we implore Thee, but sustain them by Thy Holy Spirit, and through His witness in their hearts enable them to rest in Thy fatherly love. Teach them Thy way, and lead them in a plain path. Hear our prayer, for the sake of Thy dear Son our Saviour. Amen.

[From *The Directory for Public Worship*,
The Presbyterian Church of England.]

❧ ❧ ❧ ❧

Grant, O Lord, to all who are bereaved, the spirit of faith and courage, that they may have strength to meet the days to come with steadfastness and patience, not sorrowing as those who have no hope, but in thankful remembrance of Thy great goodness in the past, and in the sure expectation of a joyful reunion in the heavenly places. This we ask in the Name of Jesus Christ our Lord. Amen.

Almighty and eternal God, who amid the changes of this mortal life art always the same, we frail children of earth do humble ourselves in Thy presence. We bow in reverence before Thy judgments, saying, "The Lord gave, and the Lord hath taken away; blessed be the Name of the Lord." In the silence of this hour speak to us of eternal things, and comfort us with the assurance of Thine everlasting love, through Jesus Christ our Lord.

God of all grace, who didst send Thy Son our Saviour Jesus Christ to bring life and immortality to light, most humbly and heartily we give Thee thanks that by His death He destroyed the power of death, and by His glorious resurrection opened the Kingdom of heaven to all believers. Grant us assuredly to know that because He lives we also shall live, and that neither death nor life, nor things present nor things to come, shall be able to separate us from Thy love which is in Him.

Help us now to wait upon Thee with reverent and submissive hearts, that as we read the words of eternal life we through patience and comfort of the Scriptures may have hope, and be lifted above our darkness and distress into the light and peace of Thy presence, through Jesus Christ our Lord. Amen.

[From *The Ordinal and Service Book*,
The Church of Scotland.]

✠ ✠ ✠ ✠

O Lord Jesus Christ, who by Thy death didst take away the sting of death, grant unto us Thy servants so to follow Thee in faith as Thou hast led the way that we may at length fall asleep peacefully in Thee, and awake after Thy likeness, through Thy mercy, who ever livest and reignest with the Father and the Holy Spirit, one God, world without end. Amen.

Father of mercies and God of all comfort, who hast brought life and immortality to light through the Gospel, we thank Thee for the messages from Thy Word and the promises that break upon our vision with the light of heavenly hope. We praise Thee for the assurance that to depart and be with Christ is far better, and that to be absent from the body is to be at home with the Lord, so that our thoughts are not turning downward to the grave but upward toward the glory. We thank Thee that "life is ever lord of death, and love can never lose its own," for since Jesus died and rose again, even so them that fall asleep in Jesus wilt Thou bring with Him, that we all may be forever with the Lord.

We thank Thee for the boundless blessings that attend our earthly pathway; in a world full of anguish our sheltered lives are brightened with sunlight and beauty. We praise Thee for the inspiration of Christian friendships; especially do we thank Thee for the one whose memory we are here to honor. For the gentleness of *his* character, the breadth of *his* sympathies, the power of *his* convictions; for *his* patience and courage, *his* genius for friendship, *his* loyalty to a great tradition; for *his* devotion to Christ and His Church—we give Thee thanks.

Now that for a time we have parted, we beseech Thee to bless the family circle that is severed, and the comrades who are bereft. Grant that we all may be worthy of our friends, and true to those who trust us. Send us back to our tasks with new cheerfulness and hope, gladly to accept whatever Thou dost give us to do or endure. As we wait for the cloudless day to dawn when the shadows shall flee away, give us unquestioning confidence in Thy holy will; and unto Thee shall be the glory forever. Amen.

[Charles R. Erdman.]

❦ ❦ ❦ ❦

Our loving Father, comfortingly look upon us in our sorrow, and abide with us in our loneliness. O Thou who makest no life in vain, and who lovest all that Thou hast made, lift upon us the light of Thy countenance, and give us peace. Amen.

We pray that Thou wilt keep in tender love the life which we shall hold in blessed memory. Help us who continue here to serve Thee with constancy, trusting in Thy promise of eternal life, that hereafter we may be united with Thy blessed children in glory everlasting, through Jesus Christ our Lord. Amen.

[From The Ritual of The Methodist Episcopal Church, 1936.]

❦ ❦ ❦ ❦

Heavenly Father, we thank Thee for that happy Home above, of which the children sing, and for that place of heavenly joy, where children with their unstained hearts grow in stature and beauty amid scenes of peace and blessedness, and where their angels do always behold the face of their Father in heaven.

We thank Thee that for a little space Thou didst grant to Thy servants this gift of Thy love, to be to them now a sanctifying and blessed memory, lifting their thoughts above the things of earth, to that abode where the child of their love is waiting to welcome them home. May this memory and hope remain with them in their hearts, and lead them to the dedication of their lives to Thee, their Father.

Help us all, O God, amid the trials and temptations of this our earthly life, to preserve within us the spirit of little children, for of such is the Kingdom of Heaven. Hear this our prayer for Jesus' sake. Amen.

[From *A New Pulpit Manual*, James Burns, editor.]

❦ ❦ ❦ ❦

Almighty God, the Father of our Lord and Saviour Jesus Christ, in this hour of sorrow, with the burden of our mortality heavy upon us, we bow before Thee. We bless Thy name for the promise of everlasting life which Thou hast given to all who believe on Jesus Christ Thy Son. Open our eyes, we beseech Thee, to behold Him present with us, as He was with sorrowing men and women in the days of His flesh, sharing their grief, comforting them in distress, revealing unto them the Father. So comfort and strengthen our faith in Him Who is the Resurrection and the Life, that neither sorrow nor death shall have dominion over us. . . .

To Thee, O Father, who pitiest Thy children, we commend those on whom this loss most sorely falls. Comfort them, we pray, as Thou alone canst comfort. Be Thou their Friend and their Helper. Grant unto them that even through their tears they may see Thy face and have assurance of Thy love. To all who are here grant Thy grace that we may learn the lessons of Thy providence. So teach us to number our days that we may apply our hearts unto wisdom.

Go with us as we are to lay this body in the ground. Let not our thoughts linger there with the dust of *him* whom we love. Rather do Thou open to us the vision of heavenly places in Christ Jesus, of the assembly of just men made perfect, where they are who have washed their robes and made them white in the blood of the Lamb, and where they ever praise Thee with unclouded vision and undivided love. All this we ask for the sake of Christ our Redeemer. Amen.

[From *The Directory for Public Worship*,
The Presbyterian Church of England.]

✤ ✤ ✤ ✤

O Lord God, Light of the faithful, Strength of the toilers, and Repose of the blessed dead, we remember before Thee all Thy servants who have departed this life in faith and fear, and especially *him* whom Thou hast now taken unto Thyself. For all Thy loving kindness to *him* throughout *his* earthly life we give Thee thanks. We bless Thee that for *him* all sickness and sorrow are ended, that death itself is past, and that *he* has entered into the rest that remaineth for Thy people, through Jesus Christ our Lord.

We beseech Thee that being inspired by the example of those who have gone before, we may run with patience the race that is set before us, looking unto Jesus, the Author and Finisher of our faith, so that when this changeful life shall have passed away we may meet with those whom Thou hast loved, in the Kingdom of Thy glory, through Jesus Christ our Lord.

Father of mercies and God of all comfort, in tender love and mercy, we beseech Thee look on Thy servants who are in sorrow. Enable them to find in Thee their Refuge and Strength, and to know the love of Christ which passeth knowledge, that their faith and hope may be in Him, who by death hath taken away the sting of death, and rising again hath opened the gates of life everlasting.

Now be with us as we follow to the grave the body of our *brother* here departed, not sorrowing as those who have no hope, but believing that as Jesus died and rose again, so them also who sleep in Jesus wilt Thou bring with Him. Amen.

[From *The Ordinal and Service Book*,
The Church of Scotland.]

✤ ✤ ✤ ✤

Almighty and eternal God, we give Thee thanks for all those redeemed by Thy grace, who, having fallen asleep in Jesus, have entered into the rest that remaineth for the children of God.

Especially do we remember Thy grace to this our *brother*, whom Thou hast taken to Thyself. We praise Thee for Thy goodness and mercy to *him*, for guidance bestowed, for strength renewed. We bless Thee for *his* knowledge of Thee, the living and true God, for *his* experience of Thy redeeming grace, and for *his* fellowship with Thy church and people.

Above all do we give thanks because Thou hast granted *him* deliverance from pain and death, and hast brought *him* from the temptations of this life to the inheritance that is incorruptible and undefiled and that fadeth not away.

Give us grace, we beseech Thee, O Lord, to be followers of them who through faith and patience have inherited the promises. Enable us also to endure unto the end, to be more than conquerors through Him that loved us, to whom be glory and praise for ever and ever. Amen.

[From *The Directory for Public Worship*,
The Presbyterian Church of England.]

❧ ❧ ❧ ❧

O Lord, support us all the day long of our troublous life, until the shadows lengthen and the evening comes, and the busy world is hushed, and the fever of life is over, and our work is done. Then in Thy mercy grant us a safe lodging, and a holy rest, and peace at the last; through Jesus Christ our Lord. Amen.

[John Henry Newman.]

❧ ❧ ❧ ❧

O the depth of the riches both of the wisdom and knowledge of God! how unsearchable are his judgments, and his ways past finding out! Rom. 11: 33.

Unto him that is able to do exceeding abundantly above all that we ask or think, according to the power that worketh in us, unto him be glory in the church by Christ Jesus throughout all ages, world without end. Amen. Eph. 3: 20, 21.

Unto the King eternal, immortal, invisible, the only wise God, be honour and glory for ever and ever. Amen. I Tim. 1: 17.

Unto him that is able to keep you from falling, and to present you faultless before the presence of his glory with exceeding joy, to the only wise God our Saviour, be glory and majesty, dominion and power, both now and ever. Amen. Jude 24, 25.

Unto him that loved us, and washed us from our sins in his own blood, and hath made us kings and priests unto God and his Father; to him be glory and dominion for ever and ever. Amen. Rev. 1: 5, 6.

The God of all grace, who hath called us unto his eternal glory by Christ Jesus, after that ye have suffered a while, make you perfect, stablish, strengthen, settle you. To him be glory and dominion for ever and ever. Amen. I Peter 5: 10, 11.

The peace of God, which passeth all understanding, keep your hearts and minds in the knowledge and love of God, and of his Son Jesus Christ; and the blessing of God Almighty, the Father, the Son, and the Holy Ghost, be amongst you and remain with you always. Amen. (Derived from Phil. 4: 7.)

The peace of our Lord Jesus Christ be with you. Amen.

The grace of our Lord Jesus Christ be with your spirit. Amen. Gal. 6: 18.

The familiar benedictions are II Cor. 13: 14; Heb. 13: 20, 21; Num. 6: 24-26.

Informational Readings

Blackwood, Andrew W., *The Fine Art of Public Worship.* The Cokesbury Press, 1939. Chapters VIII, IX.

Noyes, Morgan P., Editor, *Prayers for Services.* Charles Scribner's Sons, 1934.

Suter, John W., Editor, *The Book of English Collects.* Harper & Brothers, 1941.

X. The Formal Obituary

AMONG all the things that the minister does at a funeral, probably the least vital is the reading of the obituary. It is also the most questionable. At best the obituary is a concession to local custom. At worst the practice is far from Christian. The obituary may be a tissue of half-truths or lies. But it need never be so.

When the pastor has his heart's desire, there is no obituary. The reading of it, however brief, consumes time that is precious. The assembling of the facts may not prove easy. The phrasing of them in good literary form is much more difficult. If someone else does the writing, there may be too much or else too little. If commonplace, the production will sound flat. If well written, it may not be religious.

Nevertheless, it is possible to secure a worthy obituary. In order to prepare it aright, or else advise someone else what to include, the minister needs to ascertain facts that will later help him in making ready for the vital parts of the service..After he has thought about the obituary he is more likely to remember that in the approaching funeral there should be the human factor, as well as the divine. Into the facts as they are to appear in the obituary he can read a wealth of meaning. Shining through them all he can see the goodness of God.

The preparation of the statement calls for care in composition. There should be no attempt at appraisal of the departed, and no suggestion of a eulogy. As a rule there need be only a single, short paragraph. If the obituary is factual rather than panegyrical, it may seem cold and dull. If so, the fault may be partly in the reading. If the minister knows how to use words for the glory of God, the facts may shine.

In the family circle there may be someone who can write the obituary. If so, the minister should delegate the privilege. In such a case he leaves the content to the discretion of the writer, or else he suggests some such items as those that appear below. At the funeral, before the pastor reads the obituary, he says, "The following statement has been prepared by a friend in the family circle." If the minister himself is the author, there need be no word of explanation. In the obituary the facts are much as follows:

> The full name of the departed.
> The names of *his* father and mother.
> The place and date of *his* birth.
> The schools from which *he* graduated.
> The facts about *his* marriage (the last, if two).
> The facts about *his* children.
> The facts about *his* church life.
> The facts about *his* lifework.
> The facts about *his* military service.
> The facts about *his* fraternal affiliations.
> The time and the place of *his* death.
> The words of *his* favorite Scripture verse.
> The first stanza of *his* favorite hymn.

If the service is to include a poem this may come immediately after the obituary, thus leading up to the pastor's brief message or to the main prayer. By selecting certain hymns, as in choosing the text and the Scripture lessons, the minister can indirectly say about the departed anything that is true and worthy. Still there need be no mention of his name, except at the beginning of the obituary.

For instance, at the funeral of a schoolmaster who has been deeply beloved by successive generations of boys, the pastor might use part of the poem written by Matthew Arnold in praise of his father, Thomas Arnold, headmaster of Rugby School for Boys. Before the reading there should be a few words of explanation. Even then, the poem might be clear only to people with a rich cultural background. The words are difficult to interpret:

> "O strong soul, by what shore
> Tarriest thou now? For that force,
> Surely, has not been left vain!
> Somewhere, surely, afar,
> In the sounding labor-house vast
> Of being, is practiced that strength,
> Zealous, beneficent, firm!
>
> . . . . .
>
> "Prompt, unwearied, as here!
> Still thou upraisest with zeal
> The humble good from the ground,
> Sternly repressest the bad!
> Still, like a trumpet, dost rouse
> Those who with half-open eyes
> Tread the border-land dim
> Twixt vice and virtue; reviv'st,
> Succorest!—this was thy work;
> This was thy life upon earth.
>
> . . . . .
>
> "We were weary, and we
> Fearful, and we in our march
> Fain to drop down and to die.
> Still thou turnedst, and still
> Beckonedst the trembler, and still
> Gavest the weary thy hand.
>
> . . . . .
>
> "Strengthen the wavering line,
> Stablish, continue our march,
> On, to the bound of the waste,
> On, to the City of God."

Sometimes the indirect obituary assumes a striking form. At the Webb School in Bell Buckle, Tennessee, the idol of the boys was one of the founders, John Webb. Largely because of his influence as a teacher, more Rhodes scholars are said to have come from that school than from any other in America. When he died at an advanced age the funeral services were not sad. As they culminated at the grave and the body was being lowered to its last resting place, a group of his boys sang the hymn that he liked best: "O Love That Wilt Not Let Me Go."

At the funeral of a man less distinguished, but equally loyal to Christ and his loved ones, one might read the following tribute from a saintly widow in the second or the third century. If so, a word of explanation would be in order. The inscription appears in one of the catacombs at Rome. The translation is by Gilbert Murray. It has been slightly altered:

> "Pass hence, beloved, at the call divine,
>   Leaving the path we twain have trod;
> Pass, and the soul that still is one with thine
>   Through grief shall learn the way to God."

After the services are over, the pastor may send the family a copy of the obituary, the poem, or whatever in the service has been most distinctive and memorable. It would be easy to hand the token in person before leaving the cemetery, but there is some advantage in waiting until the morrow and then writing a note by hand, enclosing a visible evidence of the pastor's love and esteem for his friend who has fallen asleep.

The minister who day after day receives letters from near and far may not know how much it means in many a home to receive a personal message from the pastor. That is one of the countless ways in which kindness should be God's messenger of comfort. According to "Tintern Abbey," by Wordsworth, "the still, sad music of humanity" is never sweeter than in

> ". . . that best portion of a good man's life,
>   His little, nameless, unremembered acts
>   Of kindness and of love. . . ."

XI. The Elusive Poem

THE writer has long been a lover of poetry. But he questions the wisdom of using it constantly in sermons and at funerals. As a rule such effusions are of a low order as literature. Sometimes they are not delivered with distinction. Occasionally they are not clear. If so, they tend to distract. Hence there is a saying that the minister quotes poetry to please himself, not to help the people.

These observations have nothing to do with the right sort of verse. To every minister there comes a time when he is eager to lay his hands on a bit of poetry that will voice a certain mood. If only to brighten the heart of the funeral service, he may wish to read a few golden words from a master of song. The fact is that the minister with taste would read funeral poems more frequently if he could discover exactly what he desires.

At present we are to consider what a man should look for in such a poem. Later we shall think about the wisdom of the minister's having a homemade anthology. We shall assume that he already knows his hymnal better than any other book save the Bible, and that he enjoys using materials which he finds for himself. What, then, should he have in mind as he starts on his quest?

A funeral poem should be short. In the original form it may not be so. But unless the minister can use only a part, he should make some other selection. Within two or three stanzas, perhaps only one, he should be able to bring out a luminous truth, and thus give a glimpse of heavenly glory.

If it seems wise to use a part of a long poem, such as *In Memoriam,* there should be no explanation or apology. If the fragment is clear, and if it contributes to the end in view, all is well. While it would be possible to carry the idea of brevity too far, one often feels that, whether in the pulpit or at a funeral, a poem would be twice as effective if it were half as long.

But mere lack of length is not enough. There must be positive merit. It is not easy to tell what sets a worthy poem apart from prosaic rhymes. Perhaps the nearest approach is to say that a poem for use at a funeral ought to sing. The technical name for this kind of verse is a lyric. When every heart is sad, the call is for words that sing.

As a rule the poem should be fairly new to the hearers. With a hymn the reverse is often the case. In the hour of grief, if there is singing, the best is likely to be what the friends have long known and loved. The same is true of the readings from the Bible. But if there is a poem, it should be so new and pleasing that it will illumine what might otherwise be a dark corner.

The chief fact about any funeral poem is the spiritual quality. It should sing about the ways of God in the soul of man. This quality is what our twentieth-century verse most lacks. As our neighbor Albert Einstein often says about present-day music, "Much of it has no message, because there is no soul." Where some of the Victorian bards sang about the being of God and the spirit of man, the meaning of death and the hope of heaven, contemporary poets often excel in describing the petty things of earth. This is why the larger number of the poems in the anthology appended to this book are not of recent birth.

On the whole there is a vast deal of religious verse that the minister should know. Like Phillips Brooks, he may not often quote poetry in his sermons, but he should have it ever singing in his soul. He can saturate his spirit in the work of one bard after another, until he too becomes a master in the use of words. Then he will be able to read and pray out of a heart that is a wellspring of beauty.

The man who loves poetry has a soul that feels. Again he is like Phillips Brooks, who could see the promise of goodness in the heart of a little child and hear the song of the angels in a bit of fugitive verse. If in these coming days our sons keep close to the hearts of human beings, and at the same time grow in their love of beautiful words, the ministry of tomorrow should include more than a few pastors like Phillips Brooks.

There is no short cut to this kind of excellence. A man who has not as yet learned to recognize poetry when he hears it singing cannot acquire a love for the best in verse by dipping into anthologies. The richest of them, such as *The Oxford Book of Christian Verse,* should grace the shelves of a man's study. As for the "poems" that appeared in some of the older books made up for preachers, the words seldom sang. In a work that might be known as *An Up-to-Date Funeral Made to Order,* there were eighty-seven pieces of "poetry." Only two or three were able to meet the tests before us now.

THE PASTOR'S ANTHOLOGY

The part of wisdom, therefore, is for each pastor to start making his own anthology. At first he may keep in one place all sorts of religious verse; but when this part of his files begins to overflow he should set off by themselves the songs that are especially appropriate for funerals.

The best way to start a collection is to read poetry. If the quality is high, it does not matter much what the minister reads in his hours of rest. A good deal of the poetry need not be directly religious. But it should be verse about whose beauty there is no question.

For a while the minister can saturate his soul in the writings of a certain poet. It may be Dante, Milton, or Wordsworth. While the poems of Wordsworth are uneven, they contain much that the minister should know and love. In order to do so, he should read the choicest portions again and again. Better still, he should commit many of the golden words to memory.

It is good, likewise, to know the best of modern poetry, such as the work of Edwin A. Robinson or Emily Dickinson. Here too the minister finds snatches of beautiful song, though ofttimes little that is religious. In almost every magazine of the better sort there are sure to be a number of poems. Once in a while there is something that the reader wishes to preserve. If the windows of a man's soul are ever open, it is amazing how many words of beauty will keep blowing in from near and far.

After all this labor there may seem to be little fruit. With few exceptions the golden portions of Wordsworth or Milton are too long for the purpose now in view. With still fewer exceptions the excerpts from Robert Browning or John Donne will not be clear to lay friends whose favorite rhymester is Eddie Guest. No matter how lofty the song, and how much it moves the heart of the minister, if the words will not sing their way at once into the souls of the people for whom the service is being planned, the poem should have no place in the funeral service.

Nevertheless, there is value as well as joy in the quest for words that sing. Such a course of reading at home is sure to increase the sense of rhythm. That in turn affects the choice of words and the form of sentences. At Harvard, Dean L. B. R. Briggs used to say that by following a man's paper work for three or four minutes he could tell whether or not the writer had ever studied Anglo-Saxon. In like manner, by listening to a man's spoken words, especially in prayer, the discerning spirit knows whether or not the minister is a lover of poetry.

Whenever the reader discovers a treasure in verse, much of the joy comes through making it his own. One way of doing so is to write out the words and put them away with others of their kind. In the storehouse the poem may nestle for years without being used. But every once in a while the minister will take out his treasures and renew the rapture that filled his soul when he first discovered these words that sing.

The sort of poetry that a man uses at a funeral is a test of his culture. His homemade anthology likewise reveals him as a human being. After the aged minister has gone home to his God, when his loved ones turn through his papers to decide which ones to preserve, they will be wise if they keep treasures of three sorts: the pastoral prayers that he has composed, the loving letters that he has received, and the spiritual poems that he has collected if not composed. Where else on earth, save in his Bible and hymnbook, can those who tarry on in the flesh come so close to the inner spirit of the father who has fallen asleep?

Collected Poems

Cecil, Lord David, Editor, *The Oxford Book of Christian Verse.* Oxford University Press, 1940.

Clark, T. C., Compiler, *Poems for Life.* Willett, Clark & Company, 1941.

Hill, Caroline M., Editor, *The World's Great Religious Poetry.* The Macmillan Company, 1923.

XII. The Funeral Message

Is it wise to have a short funeral sermon? In each parish the answer depends largely on local custom. In one community every person expects a sermon. In an occasional Dutch congregation the tradition calls for a message that lasts thirty minutes or even longer. In another neighborhood a funeral sermon is rare. In general there is more likely to be such a message in a rural community than in a city, and in a small congregation than in a large one. But there are all sorts of exceptions.

The writer does not recommend a return to the practice of preaching at a funeral. But he feels that the minister should be ready to give a brief message whenever that seems best. In any community he should follow the best local custom. He should be especially careful to honor the most worthy traditions of his congregation. Early in each new pastorate it is good to confer with the senior elder or deacon. The response to one inquiry of the sort was as follows:

"Your predecessor almost always had something to say at a funeral. The people heard him with satisfaction, largely because they loved him. He was a man with a heart like that of God. The preceding pastor almost never spoke at a funeral. But the people said that his reading of the Scriptures and his prayers were more than enough to fill the service with light and glory. As for the neighboring ministers, most of them preach; the best of them do not. In every case do as you deem best."

In that parish the decision was not to have any funeral sermon unless there was a request from the family. With them the minister would invariably raise the question. If they thought of a funeral in terms of the former pastor who always spoke, that was the sort of service most likely to do them good. If they preferred the simple ways of the earlier minister, there was no formal message. In time the new leader began to create traditions of his own.

Before he makes any such decision, the pastor should pray. If he follows the guidance of the Holy Spirit, there may be no speaking at nine funerals out of ten, but there may be a brief sermon once in a while. "Where the Spirit of the Lord is, there is liberty" (II Cor. 3: 17). When the minister is in doubt, he had better preach. If he believes in the power of the spoken word, and if he has a healing balm for broken hearts, he may at times be glad that local custom allows him to bring words of comfort to those in distress.

Why has the funeral message been largely discontinued? The reference here is not to problem funerals; we shall think about them later. In the farewell service for a saint of God, why should there be no sermon? Doubtless because such a message in the past has not always been well prepared and properly delivered. Often it has been too long, too trite, too dull. It has seemed conventional, lifeless, impractical. In the worst sense of the word, the funeral sermon has been other-worldly.

When a minister should be his best self, he is likely to do his worst work. Time after time he may say much the same things in much the same ways and with much the same boredom. Such "sermonizing" is worth little more than it costs, which may be next to nothing. A man might as well use his breath in blowing on his hands when they are cold. If such a description seems harsh, let any pastor review some of his own preaching at funerals. Seldom does the good man have an opportunity to prepare a real message.

At the other extreme is the old-fashioned sensationalist. In most parts of the land, fortunately, he is only a local tradition. In a certain village of the Middle West a self-trained lay preacher was noted for his funeral oratory. From far and near curious folk would come to listen spellbound as he let his fancy roam through the corridors of the home on high. Despite the fact that his effusions were certain to be lengthy, the services had to be held in the largest church. As the lurid discourse went on and on, everyone kept waiting for the grand finale, which was sure to be thrilling.

For instance, take the funeral of a little girl who had met a tragic death. Near the end of the funeral discourse, in which he had recounted the details of the accident, he began to picture her as leaning from the window of her little room in the heavenly home. Through the minister, as God's messenger of mercy, she was sending words of cheer to her mother and father, her brother and sister, as well as each little playmate or friend.

Naturally there was an emotional upheaval. The man in the pulpit was so schooled that he could talk while he wept. But as he pointed to one person after another and spoke of the tender ties that had bound each heart to the little girl, the people lost control of themselves. There were constant sobs and occasional shrieks. From those nerve-racking experiences some of the victims doubtless never fully recovered. Fortunately, that kind of exhibitionism is as rare today at a funeral as in a revival service. Almost without exception, ministers now are free from such excesses.

THE SPIRIT OF THE MESSAGE

If there is a funeral message it should be worthy. What, then, are the practical tests? The most important one relates to the purpose. It is pastoral rather than evangelistic. The aim is to comfort the friends who mourn, that is, to strengthen their hearts in God. In a case where the minister can find no ground for Christian comfort, he is fortunate if he is not expected to speak.

"Whenever you preach at a funeral," said a Southern gentlewoman to the pastor of a neighboring church, "you always try to bring the comfort of God." The minister expressed his thanks, and then he asked, "Pardon me, but what else could I attempt to do?" "I scarcely know," was the reply, "but you are the only clergyman in town who always uses a funeral service as a means of bringing Christian comfort."

The spirit of such a message is like that of the meditation prior to the Lord's Supper. In each case, if there is anything approaching a sermon, it should be short and full of meaning as well as of light and beauty. The appeal should be mainly to the heart, not the head. In this respect many a funeral message misses the mark. It is coldly intellectual. It attempts to prove what the heart already feels. There is little appeal to what Bunyan calls the ear-gate. Such a sermon would be better if left unspoken.

The funeral message ought to be short. Even at the services in memory of a lay officer in the church, ten minutes may be the upper limit for the sermon. As a rule six or eight minutes should prove ample. Still there need be no appearance of haste. There is no time for a preamble. The occasion calls for only a single truth. That one should shine. If it is about "Heaven as Home," there need be no proof, no argument, no elaboration. The reliance should be on the words of the Lord Jesus: "In my Father's house are many mansions" (John 14: 2). In terms of today one can use a paraphrase: "In the Father's home there are many rooms."

Whatever the minister says at a funeral should be interesting. In this respect the call may be for something like a junior sermon. When grief fills the hearts of men and women, they often become as meek as little boys and girls. There is a clear pathway into every heart. The door is open wide. Without taking time to arouse interest, the pastor begins at once to use divine truth in meeting human needs. From the opening words to the closing syllable, his heart is speaking to their hearts. "Deep soundeth unto deep."

Think of a specific case. A boy twelve years of age had always been frail. He was the only child, and because of his birth there could never be another babe. For the lad's sake the parents had moved to the suburbs, where they had built a home, so that he could play in the sunshine. Gradually he was growing more robust. But one morning, while taking his bath, he was electrocuted. He died at once. In making ready for the funeral the pastor found that the father and the mother wished a brief message.

The question was how to bring them comfort. If the minister had stressed the facts in the case there would have been needless anguish. At last he determined to start with the text: "The broad places of the city shall be filled with boys and girls playing in the broad places thereof" (Zech. 8: 5, in the orginal). Strictly interpreted, that text does not refer to heaven. Nevertheless, the striking words enabled the pastor to make clear what was in his heart. He spoke about the City of God as a place of beauty where the heavenly Father knows how to make a growing boy feel at home from the very first. In the Father's house everyone is well and strong, being filled with the spirit of eternal youth.

The appeal should be mainly to the imagination. In a few minutes there is time for only a single truth. It should be luminous. It should appeal to the friends where they are, in a home that seems to have lost its reason for being. The message should lead them to lift up their hearts unto God. The healing grace is in him, and in his promises.

Since the time is short, there should be little exegesis, and no argument. Even if there were time for a logical discourse about immortality, the hearers would be in no condition to think hard and long. But still their eyes may be open, perhaps as never before. Both in the text and in the words that follow there should be something for them to see and feel. There should also be something tangible that they will remember. Whatever the circumstances, there is always some word from God for those who need him sorely.

For example, at the funeral of an aged farmer the dominant note may be that of the harvest. If the deceased has been

a godly leader, an officer in the church, the minister can
have the people rise to sing,

> " 'Come, ye thankful people, come,
>   Raise the song of harvest home.' "

In the sermon the text may be one of the many that speak
about death in terms of gathering the harvest, e.g., Gen. 15:
15 or Job 5: 26. Ideally, the resulting message should be
somewhat like a lyric poem.

The funeral sermon ought to have a beauty all its own.
Throughout the service, from the organ prelude to the benediction, and beyond that to what is done at the grave, everything should move in the realm of mystic beauty. In all that
the Bible teaches about the death of the believer there is
naught save beauty. Everything relating to ugliness is of
the earth earthy, and that has all been done away through
the death of Christ. To be in keeping with the facts, the
farewell message should be radiant with the beauty of the
Lord.

From one funeral to another the shades of beauty should
vary. In a bed of pansies the appeal to the heart is not the
same as in a bank of climbing roses. In a farewell service for
a little girl the tone color should be different from that when
her grandfather has fallen asleep at the end of golden years.
"There is one glory of the sun, and another glory of the
moon, and another glory of the stars: for one star differeth
from another star in glory. So also is the resurrection of the
dead" (I Cor. 15: 41, 42).

THE CHOICE OF THE TEXT

At least among friends who love the Lord, the easiest way
to start well is to quote a text. Nothing else on earth is so
sure to touch and move the heart as a few words from
mother's Bible. Just as in singing the hymn "Holy, Holy,
Holy," the first six notes of the melody sound the motif of
it all, so in a funeral message the opening words from the

Bible should voice the dominant theme. As long as any hearer lives, these words from the Book should keep ringing through his soul.

It may not prove easy to select a passage that is sure to meet the needs of the approaching hour. In one case the text may come to mind without effort. Again, the pastor must search and be patient. But if he knows the Book, and if he waits upon the Lord, in due time the text will appear. When once it knocks at the door, there need be no question about credentials. Neither should there be any thought about a second choice. When once the golden text has found its way into the heart of the preacher, the work of preparing the message has well begun.

As a rule the text should be short. Provided it makes complete sense, the shorter the text, the more it will shine. For instance, if the friends are in love with the sea, they will respond to words about hope as "an anchor of the soul" (Heb. 6: 19). In such a case the idea is to interpret the figure as it sets forth the facts, and then to speak of the facts in the light of the figure. The reference is to the olden time when every vessel of any size had sails.

When a large ship drew near to a harbor that was difficult to enter, the captain would send a seaman ahead in a little boat. Within the bay he would drop the anchor, to which was attached a rope extending back to the ship. Then little by little the sailors on board would draw the vessel safely into the harbor. Thus it should be in the Christian life. Within the haven our Forerunner, Jesus Christ, has gone to drop the anchor. Day by day we should be drawing nearer to the time when we shall be with him beyond the reach of earthly storms. Meanwhile we should work out our own salvation, with fear and trembling.

As a rule the text should be more nearly self-evident. If it is not clear and luminous, one should make it so with a few simple sentences; otherwise, it is better to choose some passage that is more obvious. If the words are in the form of a question, it should be clear. For instance, "If a man die, shall he live again?" (Job 14: 14). Whatever the text, there is little time for interpretation. In other sorts of preaching there is a place for careful instruction, but in a funeral sermon the chosen words should shine in their own light.

The text should be striking. It should arrest attention, and fix itself at once in the memory. Even if the friends are all worn out, after weeks of anxious waiting followed by hours of frenzied activity, they should respond to a striking text. So it ought to be in the funeral of a soldier: "If this earthly tent is taken down, we have a building of God, a house not made with hands, eternal in the heavens" (II Cor. 5: 1, in the original). The figure may be that of a soldier who for months has been living in a tent. At last the call comes to fold up the tent and sail home.

Such a text appeals to the imagination. It makes the hearer think of death as the supreme adventure. He should look forward to the hour when he too shall hear the call, "Westward-ho!" If there were time for a teaching sermon it might be about the resurrection of the body or, rather, the glory of the heavenly abode. But since the time is brief, all that the minister can do is to leave in the waiting heart the picture of the life everlasting as the home of the warrior.

In the classic chapter about the life to come there are many striking texts. One of them speaks about dying as putting off earthly garments, and about entrance into the other world as putting on heavenly attire. "This corruptible must put on incorruption, and this mortal must put on immortality" (I Cor. 15: 53).

When such words start to sing in the hearer's soul they will suggest to him far more than the minister has time to say. They should help the man in sorrow to feel sure that from a mortal body, with all its frailties and shortcomings, the loved one has gone to be with the Father God. What He has in store for his children in the world to come no person here can begin to tell. But this we know: the One who fashioned our present bodies is able to prepare something better by far in a world where sin never dares to enter. He knows how to make heaven seem like home, and how to make us worthy to dwell with him and his saints forevermore.

THE FORM OF THE MESSAGE

The form of any funeral sermon must depend in part on the length of time that the minister has for preparation. If in a single day he must speak at two or three funerals, each of which calls for a sermon of a different kind, obviously he cannot make ready as he desires. But in the farewell service for a beloved officer in the church, who has been wasting away for weeks, there is every reason why the pastor should be prepared.

The style of the message should be that of quiet charm. If everything else in the service has a beauty not of earth, the pastor's sermon ought also to be

> "Instinct with loveliness, and sweet and rare,
> The perfect emblem of its Maker's care."

Especially should he be watchful about the first few sentences. They should flow from the text and have much the same tone color. In fact, the entire message should have a pleasing rhythm. When the heart of the pastor is being moved, his words ought to have a rhythm like that of the King James Bible. So they will if he knows how to write and speak.

The effectiveness of the funeral sermon depends much upon the delivery. If the services are in a private home, and if the friends are seated in another room, there is no reason why he should not read the most vital parts of the message. But in the sanctuary, or whenever the members of the family are looking up into the face of their pastor and friend, with the hope of catching a glimpse of light from God, there ought to be no glancing down at a notebook. Especially since the sermon is brief and simple, one should be able to talk without any "helps."

In a funeral message the voice ought to be audible but it should never seem loud. The rate of utterance should be deliberate without seeming to be slow. At times the way of speaking should attain distinction. If ever on earth a man is able to serve as a herald of the King, it should be in the presence of death. The need is evident, as the friends look to him for the light that he alone can bring. The message is in his heart, for it has come from the Book. All that he needs now is unction from the Most High God.

From one funeral to another, at least within the congregation, there should be a wholesome variety of messages. If at times the minister follows a familiar trail, the people will understand. But in view of the manifold needs of human hearts, and the boundless resources within the Bible, there seldom needs to be any sameness that will call attention to itself. In order to keep from saying much the same things again and again, the pastor ought to form the habit of preparing messages to meet human needs.

The current name for this kind of preaching is the "life situation sermon." While the name is new, the idea is not. Some of us have been doing this kind of sermonic work for years. We prefer to call it "divine power for human needs." Whatever the title, such preaching is in order whenever there is a call for a funeral message. If any minister wishes to become a master in the art of preparing "life situation sermons," the secret is simple. Live by faith, and learn by doing.

XIII. The Sermonic Seed Plot

IN A parish where every funeral calls for a brief message, how does the minister find his materials? Partly by preaching from the Bible, and also by being forehanded. No matter how many calls there may be, and how many people are present at almost every funeral, there is always something new to say. The pastor needs to think of only one sermon at a time. For that one he should trust in the God who has stood by him before.

Ofttimes the minister scarcely knows how he first discovered the text that leads to the funeral sermon. The seed thought may have come during one of the visits at the bedside of the dying friend, or else in the later interview with the family. The idea may have emerged while they were telling him the facts for the obituary. Just as in a coal country every boy knows the meaning of the "blossom" on the hillside, so in our calling the minister often says to himself: "If I dig into that bank I shall get what I need." All that he finds necessary is a "lead."

Sometimes the sermonic idea has to do with the season of the year. If the time is just before Christmas or Easter, the thought of the Incarnation or the Resurrection will help the friends to find peace in the face of the last great mystery. During the spring one can speak about the seedtime, and in the autumn there is the glory of the harvest. In the depths of winter, everyone can behold "The Gospel in the Snow." It affords a way of contact between the sorrowing hearts and the God who sends the snow.

It is good, also, to consider the lifework of the deceased. Without descending to personalities, the minister can speak

of religion and the life everlasting in terms of the builder or
the athlete, the soldier or the sailor, the musician or the traveling man, the schoolmaster or the housemother. Again, the
facts about the departed may suggest the crossing of a river
or the sailing of a ship, the moving to a new home or the
return to an old one, the coming of sleep or the sowing of
seed for the eternal harvest.

When once the facts about the deceased have suggested
the trail that the minister is to follow, his problem should
be transformed into an opportunity. For instance, take the
idea of a voyage. This is how the truth shone out in a
sermon by an old-fashioned preacher who loved to journey
through Eastern waters:

"We make too much of death. We do not dwell enough
on the soul and its ongoing might. As one sails the Mediter-
ranean, round whose shores much that is greatest in history
has taken place, one shrinks from leaving it. Then too the
sea contracts toward the west; the shores gather together;
in the way of the ongoing mariner the straits are narrow;
apparently they are impassable; they are like the end of a
man's life.

"But as you advance, the illusion vanishes. The straits are
wide enough for the mightiest ship. On past the great rocks
at the portal, your ship goes out into the vaster sea. From
the horizon comes the call of loved ones, and the tender
welcome home.

"Such is a man's voyage on the sea of time. In the narrow
passage there is room for the greatest soul. Let him go forward in confidence and hope. Beyond is the Infinite, and out
into it the soul is moving to find the welcome of the Father's
love and the light of his eternal home."

In this kind of semipoetic preaching a man should be on
his guard. Otherwise he may follow his fancy and depart
from good taste. For example, think of the funeral service
in memory of a church officer who for years had been worthy
of note for loyalty and meekness. The choice of the text was

worthy: "Well done, good and faithful servant" (Matt. 25: 23). But the dominant figure was open to question. The minister had recently returned from a trip to the Northwest, and he spoke about the departed in terms of "Old Faithful." Some of those present could not see the resemblance between the layman who had been notable for humility and a geyser that intermittently spouts hot water.

THE SEED PLOT

The minister is less likely to depart from good taste if he lets the seed thought grow for weeks or months before he brings it out in public. Whenever an idea relating to death or the hereafter comes into mind, the part of wisdom is to put the seed thought away to mature. In the homiletical garden the idea may grow for years. When at last the need arises, the resulting message will have back of it all that long brooding. In such a case the work of preparation may call for only a little time and energy.

The following suggestions have to do with starting a seed plot for funeral sermons. In any one example the writer could indicate how he would deal with the germinal thought. But such a development might deprive someone else of the joy that comes through thinking for himself. If any minister wishes to find satisfaction in the hours of study, he should use his intellectual muscles. Then the funeral message will come chiefly from the Book, and will meet the needs of burdened hearts.

After he becomes accustomed to working this way, any thoughtful pastor can make a seedbed of his own. Culture of such a garden will enrich his whole ministry and make him more Christlike.

The Funeral of a Child

I Sam. 1: 28a.   The Giving of a Child to God.
II Sam. 12: 23c.   The Hope of a Reunion in Heaven.
Isa. 11: 6c.   The Influence of a Little Child.

Isa. 40: 11.	The Shepherd with His Lambs.
Matt. 18: 2.	The Lover of Little Children.
Matt. 19: 14.	The Friend of Little Children.

Of a Boy or a Girl

II Kings 4: 26c.	The Death of a Growing Boy.
Zech. 8: 5.	The Joys of Children in Heaven.
Luke 8: 52.	The Meaning of Death as Sleep.

Of a Youth or a Maiden

Gen. 22: 12.	The Love of a Father for His Son.
I Sam. 20: 18b.	The Vacant Chair in the Home.
Job 1: 21.	The Grief of a Father for His Sons.
Eccl. 12: 1.	The Meaning of a Young Man's Religion.
Luke 7: 14.	The Sympathy of the Lord Jesus.
I John 2: 14b.	The Glory of Young Manhood.

Of One of Middle Age

Job. 19: 25a.	The Hope of a Personal Resurrection.
Ps. 90: 12.	The Passing of the Years.
Matt. 11: 28-30.	The Gift of Rest for the Soul.
Matt. 12: 20.	The Compassion of the Lord Jesus.
Matt. 20: 12b.	The Laborers in God's Vineyard.
John 11: 25, 26.	The Giver of Life Everlasting.
John 14: 27.	The Secret of the Untroubled Heart.
I Cor. 15: 58.	The Power of Christian Hope.
Rev. 14: 13.	The Reward of Work Done for God.

Of One Who Is Old

Gen. 5: 24.	The Joys of Walking with God.
Gen. 15: 15.	The Gathering of the Heavenly Harvest.
Num. 23: 10b.	The Death of the Godly Man.
Ps. 90: 17.	The Beauty of God's Older Children.
Ps. 91: 16.	The Glory of a Godly Old Age.
Luke 2: 29.	The Prayer of an Aged Believer.
Phil. 1: 21.	The Joys of Being with the Lord.
II Tim. 4: 7, 8.	The Faith of a Christian Veteran.

Of One Who Has Suffered Long

Deut. 33: 27a.	The Secret of Security in God.
Job 1: 21.	The Afflictions of a Godly Man.
Ps. 16: 11.	The Joys of the Life to Come.
Rom. 8: 18.	The Contrast Between Earth and Heaven.
Rom. 8: 28.	The Basis of Christian Optimism.
II Cor. 4: 7.	The Glory of Earthen Vessels.
Rev. 7: 14.	The Cleansing Power of Christ.
Rev. 7: 17.	The Felicity of the Redeemed.

Of One Who Has Been Friendly

I Sam. 18: 1.	The Pattern of Abiding Friendship.
II Sam. 1: 26.	The Glory of Human Friendship.
John 11: 11b.	The Friend of the Master.
John 15: 15.	The Meaning of Religion as Friendship.

Of a Pious Father

Gen. 18: 19.	The Best Thing About a Good Father.
Ex. 20: 12.	The Way to Honor a Father.
I Kings 2: 2, 3a.	The Spirit of a Father's Loyalty.
II Kings 2: 9c.	The Mantle of a Father's Service.
Ps. 103: 13.	The Sympathy of the Father God.
Isa. 38: 1b.	The Way to Prepare for Death.
John 14: 2.	The Hospitality of Heaven.
Heb. 12: 1, 2a.	The Inspiration from the Departed.

Of a Godly Mother

Prov. 31: 30, 31.	The Bible Picture of a Godly Mother.
Isa. 66: 13.	The Loving Kindness of Mother's God.
John 14: 2.	The Welcome to the Heavenly Home.
II Tim. 1: 5.	The Influence of a Pious Mother.

Of a Godly Farmer

Job 5: 26.	The Farmer's Hope of Heaven.
Ps. 1: 3.	The Fruitfulness of a Godly Life.

Micah 6: 8.	The Religion of a Farmer.
John 12: 24.	The Seed Corn of Heaven.
I Cor. 15: 20.	The Beginning of the Eternal Harvest.

Of a Christian Businessman

Matt. 6: 19, 20.	The Treasures of a Good Man's Heart.
Matt. 25: 21.	The Rewards of Faithful Service.
Phil. 1: 21.	The Inventory of a Good Man's Life.
James 4: 14b.	The Mist on God's Mountain.

Of Some Other Friends

I Sam. 20: 3c.	A Victim of Foul Play.
Mal. 2: 5-7.	The Pastor of the Church.
Matt. 25: 23.	The Religion of the Average Man.
Matt. 25: 34.	The Rewards of Christian Kindness.
John 11: 3.	The Brother in the Christian Home.
John 11: 28.	The Sister in the Godly Home.
Acts 6: 5b.	The Religion of a Deacon.
I Peter 5: 4.	The Elder in the Church.
Dan. 12: 3.	The Rewards of the Godly Teacher.
(R. V., margin)	

A Cluster of Golden Texts

Ps. 23: 6.	The Joys of the Heavenly Home.
Ps. 116: 15.	The Death of God's Saints.
Ps. 127: 2b.	The Sleep of God's Beloved.
Mal. 3: 17.	The Jewels of the Lord.
Matt. 6: 20.	The Treasures of God's Children.
II Cor. 5: 4.	The Garments of Immortality.
I Tim. 4: 8.	The Rewards of Godliness.
I Tim. 6: 19.	The Foundations of Life Eternal.
Heb. 13: 14.	The City of the Redeemed.
Rev. 21: 4.	The City Without Tears.
Rev. 21: 25.	The Gates of the Heavenly City.
Rev. 22: 5.	The City of Everlasting Light.

XIV. The Sunlit Grave

THE funeral services ought to reach their climax at the grave. All that has gone before should lead up to the final emphasis on the resurrection of the body and the life everlasting. In this assurance everyone present should join. On all sides are the resting places of departed friends. To the redeemed children of God even the gloomiest tombstones ought to serve as emblems of eternal life. It was so in the catacombs at Rome.

At the cemetery the setting is usually one of beauty. The place of burial is likely to be among the hills. Here and there are trees. On every hand there is grass, and in the summer there are flowers. Far in the distance may be a river, which makes one think of the trumpet sounding for Bunyan's Pilgrim. Perhaps the sun is about to set. In all God's outer world everything saith, "Glory!"

Despite the beauty of the background, the services are sometimes disappointing. Occasionally they are almost pagan. More often they are perfunctory. If there is dignity, there may be coldness, as well as stiffness. The prevailing spirit may be that of unreality. The burial rites over a saint may be the same as for a scoundrel. In recent years, however, there has been a marked improvement. If at times there is still something unseemly, it is doubtless due to lack of taste or of proper training.

Thus far we have assumed that the minister in charge of the services elsewhere should also be God's spokesman at the grave. Some books suggest that he ask to be excused. If that is necessary, because the parish is vast or because he is feeble, everyone will understand. But if he is able to be with the family at the cemetery, he can invest an hour or two most profitably. There is no easy pathway to being a good minister of Jesus Christ.

At the grave the length of the services should depend in part upon the weather. The suggestions here relate to a time of year when the air is balmy and to an hour of the day when the sun is shining. In such a case there is no reason for cutting the services short. There is time for a well-rounded ritual, which ought to be climactic. The idea is to send everyone home thinking about life instead of death, and the joys of heaven rather than the desolateness of earth. Throughout every syllable the services ought to be vibrant with Biblical energy and luminous with Christian hope.

The exercises need not last longer than five or six minutes. When the weather is foul the time should be shorter. Once in a blizzard, when the thermometer stood at zero, the writer simply pronounced the benediction. The way to show respect for the dead is to have concern for the living. Otherwise a single funeral may lead to a number of deaths. Physically, people are in no condition to withstand exposure. Even if there is a canopy over the grave, some may become chilled if the services last more than a very few minutes, the fewer the better.

Whenever the clergyman deems it wise to depart from custom because of inclement weather he should consult beforehand with one or more of the family. Whereas it is customary for the minister, as well as the other men, to stand at the grave with head uncovered, that would be foolhardy when there is rain or snow. Through the mortician the pastor can notify the pallbearers that they are free to wear their hats. They will be relieved to learn that common sense prevails.

At the historic Princeton Cemetery on a wintry afternoon Clarence E. Macartney, of Pittsburgh, stood by the grave of his predecessor and personal friend, Maitland Alexander. Assisting in the service was President John A. Mackay, of

Princeton Seminary. Without explanation or apology each of
them wore his hat. That was a present-day version of the
Golden Rule.

Whatever the weather, the minister should be at hand
when the pallbearers remove the casket from the funeral
carriage. When they are ready to move he should walk
slowly with the mortician as together they lead the procession. At the grave the minister stands a little to one side until
the pallbearers have deposited the casket on the descending
device. Meanwhile he should have ascertained from the
mortician which is the head of the grave. As a rule that is
where he stands. However, if the mortician suggests otherwise, it makes no difference.

When everything is ready the mortician indicates that the
clergyman is to take charge. A good way to begin is to read
the One Hundred and Twenty-first Psalm. Afterward, if the
departed has been a Christian, it is good to repeat Rev. 14:
13. Meanwhile the mortician is beside the grave. He is waiting to strew on the casket either flowers or dust. As he does
so, the minister slowly repeats the committal service. In an
occasional service the people prefer that there be no such
form of committal. If so, one can substitute a reading from
the New Testament, e.g., Rev. 21: 1-7 or ch. 22: 1-5. Some
of us think that this sort of reading is much better than the
stereotyped committal ceremony.

When custom calls for words of committal it is more
effective to recite than to read from a book. No matter how
many funerals there may be, with some of the same people
present almost every time, the pastor needs to vary the form
of committal only when the deceased has not been known as
a consistent Christian. Then, if the matter were not serious,
one might say facetiously that the words of farewell should
be "noncommittal." The following is one of various forms
that are suitable when the departed has been an unbeliever:

"Here we commit the body to its kindred dust—earth to
earth, ashes to ashes, dust to dust. The spirit we leave with

God. May the living lay it to heart. As we know that God
will bring us every one to the grave, let us here dedicate
ourselves to do with our might what our hands find to do.
May our trust be in Him who says, 'I am the resurrection,
and the life: he that believeth in me, though he were dead,
yet shall he live: and whosoever liveth and believeth in me
shall never die.' "

In the burial of a believer, after the committal service may
come the Apostles' Creed, in which everyone present should
join. During the committal ceremony and the recitation of
the Creed it is wise to keep the loose-leaf notebook open at
the proper page. Then if the memory falters, as it may, the
thing to do is to read until the trail again becomes clear.
If one is speaking deliberately, an involuntary pause may be
impressive. But as a rule there need be no such interrup-
tion. If all goes well the saying of the Creed in unison may
be the climactic part of the entire ceremony.

After the Creed there should be a prayer. It need not be
long. The underlying truth may be the assurance of the resurrection. On this basis, because the Lord Jesus arose from the
tomb and is alive forevermore, the minister should lead his
friends as one by one they dedicate themselves anew to the
service of God, who alone can make anyone feel secure about
the resurrection of the body and the life everlasting.

If the services elsewhere have not included The Lord's
Prayer, it may come now. In the spirit of the familiar words,
"Thy will be done in earth, as it is in heaven," the people
should be ready to receive the benediction. At times it may
be better to use some other form, such as the Apostolic
Benediction, but as a rule the Covenant Benediction (Heb.
13: 20, 21) seems to be most fitting at the grave.

When it is spoken aright, this unique benediction may be
more moving than a sermon. The words of blessing actually
bestow on the hearts of believers the covenant mercies of the
Almighty: "The God of peace, that brought again from the
dead our Lord Jesus, that great shepherd of the sheep,

through the blood of the everlasting covenant, make you
perfect in every good work to do his will, working in you
that which is wellpleasing in his sight, through Jesus Christ;
to whom be glory for ever and ever. Amen."

In most communities, after the benediction it is the custom
for the members of the family circle to go at once to their
carriages. If they prefer to tarry for a while and mingle with
loved ones who have come home from afar, the pastor should
not interfere. But if there is any evidence of uncertainty
about what is proper, he should offer to escort them to the
waiting vehicles. He should know, as they do not, that the
mortician has work to do elsewhere. The minister, likewise,
has calls to make at the hospital. Then, too, the people most
concerned need to go home, where they can relax.

In an occasional community, however, the custom may
be different. In certain parts of the South, whenever the skies
are balmy, the funeral party tarries near the grave until it is
filled. Meanwhile there may be quiet snatches of conversation, but as a rule everyone is silent. The minister should not
talk. When everything is in readiness, loving hands drape
the sunlit mound with flowers fresh from the gardens back
at home. Then as the loved ones depart from the cemetery
their last recollections of the services are in terms of beauty.

At such an impressive funeral the filling of the grave may
come immediately after the psalm and the committal service.
Then the Apostles' Creed and the short pastoral prayer, with
the benediction, should be the culminating part of the exercises. When all these things are ordered aright, this sort of
ceremony is the most memorable that the writer has witnessed
at the grave.

PRAYERS USED AT THE GRAVE

Heavenly Father, look in mercy upon these our friends as
they leave the earthly form of their loved one resting beneath
the beauty of Thy flowers. Be with these Thy children as they
go again to their home. Grant them faith to believe in the com-

munion of saints, the forgiveness of sins, the resurrection of
the body, and the life everlasting. Through Thy Spirit enable
them to be steadfast, unmoveable, always abounding in the
work of the Lord, forasmuch as they know that their labor is
not in vain in the Lord (I Cor. 15: 58).

[Adapted.]

❦ ❦ ❦ ❦

Almighty God, who by the death of Thy dear Son hast destroyed death, by His rest in the tomb hast sanctified the graves
of Thy saints, and by His glorious resurrection hast brought
life and immortality to light; receive, we beseech Thee, our un-
feigned thanks for that victory over death and the grave which
He hath obtained for us and for all who sleep in Him; and
keep us ever in communion with those who await Thee here
upon earth and with those who stand around Thy throne in
heaven: in union with Him who is the Resurrection and the
Life, who liveth and reigneth with Thee and the Holy Spirit,
ever one God, world without end. Amen.

[From *The Ordinal and Service Book*, The
Church of Scotland.]

❦ ❦ ❦ ❦

Grant, O Lord, to all who are bereaved, the spirit of faith and
courage, that they may have strength to meet the days to come
with steadfastness and courage; not sorrowing as those without
hope, but in thankful remembrance of Thy great goodness in
past years, and in the sure expectation of a joyful reunion in the
heavenly places; and this we ask in the Name of Jesus Christ
our Lord. Amen.

[From *The Book of Common Prayer* According to
the Use of the Church of England in Ireland.]

XV. The Possible Cremation

EVERY minister should be familiar with the facts about cremation. The term relates to the practice of committing the body
to the flames and then preserving the ashes. Another term is
incineration. In that process, which is not so common as
cremation, the body is exposed to intense heat, but not directly to the flames. The final effect is the same. By weight
ninety-seven per cent of the body disappears in the form of
vapors; three per cent remains in the form of gray ashes.

The place where all these rites occur is called a crematory.
The receptacle for the ashes is an urn. The place where the
urns repose is a columbarium. Literally the word means a
resting place for doves. In Roman history the columbarium
was a vault lined with recesses for cinerary urns. Anyone who
visits an up-to-date columbarium will see the resemblance to
a vast dovecote. Ordinarily the crematory and the columbarium are housed beneath a single roof.

It is worth any young minister's while to visit such an
establishment. In Greater New York there is one at Ferncliff,
near Ardsley, in Westchester County. In the suburbs of almost every large city there is a like institution. In the Far
West the practice of cremation is more common than in the
East or the South. But now that cemeteries are becoming
crowded, and it is legally impossible to set apart land for
these purposes within the limits of a city like New York,
there will likely be an increasing trend toward cremation.

Personally, the minister may or may not approve of such
proceedings. Privately, he is free to hold any opinion that he
will. But officially he should keep an open mind. In the
Christian religion there is nothing that frowns upon crema-

tion or requires burial. If a body is lost at sea or consumed in a burning building, the remains are still in the keeping of the Father God. So it is if the relatives prefer cremation in lieu of burial; they alone have the right to determine the disposition of the dear body.

Sooner or later a minister is likely to be consulted about the services over a body that is to be cremated, or else about what to do with the ashes that remain. There is no special difficulty about his part in such services. The reason for discussing the matter now is to forestall any feeling of uncertainty or dread. As a young clergyman approaches his first ceremony of the sort, let him trust in God and not be afraid.

The difficulties are chiefly psychological. The minister who has always thought of death as leading to burial may find in these other circumstances nothing but unreality. If so, let him remember three truths. Each is spiritual and vital.

First, God is as near to sorrowing people in a columbarium as at a cemetery. Secondly, his children are as much in need of comfort before and after the cremation of the body as though it were to be buried. Thirdly, the minister of the Gospel should fix his eyes on the things that are unseen and eternal. Thus only can he bring to needy hearts the solace that comes from the Father God, through the old, old way of the Cross, which is ever new.

When the body is to be cremated the services may be held at the residence the evening before. That time of day is convenient for all concerned. If the throng is likely to be large the exercises may be held elsewhere. For some reason, however, a church funeral almost never occurs after dark. Hence the services there might be late in the afternoon.

Whatever the time and the place, the exercises are much the same as though the body were to be buried. Instead of having the final services at the grave, however, they are at the columbarium. They are held, as a rule, after the cremation, and are private. If the pastor's other engagements permit, he plans to be with the friends when they go to the crematory.

He makes a special effort to be with them when they put the urn in the columbarium. Any such ceremony must be at an hour when the gates are open and the attendants are on duty.

Still another plan is to hold the chief funeral services in the chapel under the same roof as the crematory and the columbarium. What the minister says and does in the chapel is much the same as at a funeral parlor. If he thinks about the matter calmly, and makes his plans carefully, all should go well. After the services are over he may wonder at his previous perturbation.

What the minister says and does at the columbarium is much the same as at a grave. However, it is advisable to make a few slight alterations in the committal service. When the exercises are held before the cremation the Scottish *Book of Common Order* suggests the following:

"Forasmuch as it hath pleased Almighty God to take unto Himself the soul of our *brother* here departed, we therefore commit *his* body to be dissolved, ashes to ashes, dust to dust, in sure and certain hope of the resurrection to eternal life, through our Lord Jesus Christ."

When the ceremony takes place after the cremation the same rites will serve, with a single change. Instead of saying, "We therefore commit *his* body to be dissolved," the minister declares, "We therefore commit *his* ashes to this resting-place." In no case should there be any use of the word "flame," or "fire."

If the deceased has been a Christian, the minister may add these triumphant words from the Apocalypse: "I heard a voice from heaven saying unto me, Write, Blessed are the dead which die in the Lord from henceforth: Yea, saith the Spirit, that they may rest from their labours; and their works do follow them" (Rev. 14: 13).

XVI. The Fraternal Order

SOMETIMES there is a question concerning the part in the services to be taken by a fraternal order. If the deceased has been a member of the Masons, or some other secret society, the family may wish the lodge officials to share in the public exercises. If so, the minister should gladly assent to whatever the people desire. If their spokesman is not aware of what is customary, the pastor should explain the possibilities. The decision about what to do, however, should rest with the family. Obviously, the rest of this chapter applies to only an occasional funeral.

In most communities the custom now is for the lodge to have services in the home, or at the funeral parlors, on the evening prior to the day for the exercises conducted by the pastor. The notice about the lodge services appears in the daily newspapers. The officers and members can be present without losing time from their regular work. The chaplain of the lodge is more likely to be available than at the funeral on the following day. As a result, there are two distinct services, which differ in character. Each of them may be almost a model of its kind.

Another plan is still less common. In it the representatives of the lodge share with the minister in the exercises at the home, the church, or the funeral parlors. In such a case the lodge officials usually prefer to come last. If so, the clergyman carries out his part in the services and then gives way to the official who is to assume charge. Of course the clergyman keeps his part of the exercises fairly short. He should also do his best to make them shine. He does not wish to have the Church overshadowed.

At the proper time it is the part of courtesy for the minister to introduce the chief representative of the lodge. Previously these two should have held a private conference. In it the pastor should have written down the requisite facts. Then he can state them with clarity and precision. The announcement may be as follows: "The remainder of the services will be in charge of Mercer Lodge Number Fifty, Free and Accepted Masons, under the leadership of the Grand Master." During these ceremonies the minister should remain, giving reverent attention to all that is said and done.

Another procedure is even less common of late. It is for the lodge to take part only at the grave. In fact, the officials may be willing to excuse the clergyman from attendance at the cemetery. The fraternal burial rites are often impressive, not to say spectacular. That is likely to be the case when the Knights Templars perform. On each side of the grave stands a row of comrades, with swords upraised and crossed, thus forming an arch of steel athwart the open tomb. Then the chaplain intones the stately ritual. If he has a sense of rhythm and knows how to read, the effect may be picturesque.

Friction between the minister and the officials of the lodge is most likely to occur with reference to the benediction at the grave. Just as professing Christians in the Holy Land quarrel about the reputed sites of the Saviour's birth and death, so do his followers in our homeland sometimes squabble about the holiest words that mortal lips can utter. Fortunately, such spectacles are rare today. If the lodge officials like the minister personally, they usually ask him to pronounce the benediction. If they prefer to have it spoken by their own chaplain, who may not have been ordained, why should there be any dispute? At the grave let there be peace and good will among men.

In this connection it is interesting to note the official regulations for chaplains in the Army. At a military funeral the regular services by the grave precede the rites of any fraternal organization. If the lodge ceremonies are semi-military, they come immediately after the Army religious service. Then there may be the firing of muskets and the sounding of taps. Nonmilitary rites conducted by a fraternal organization are held at the conclusion of taps. Since the Army services may be in the hands of a civilian clergyman, if the family so desires, it is clear that the Army gives the place of prominence to the regular religious exercises.

However, it is not wise for a minister of the Gospel to be concerned about his personal "rights." If he is tactful and considerate he need anticipate no difficulty in making satisfactory arrangements with the officers of any recognized fraternal order. With few exceptions they are Christian gentlemen. They have worthy ideals, as well as tolerance. Unfortunately, they must sometimes deal with a clergyman who is unwilling to budge an inch, or even allow them a minute of "his" time, as though he were the Almighty! Since no rites can make any difference to the deceased, both pastor and lodge officials should accede to what the family desires.

The occasional clergyman does not understand how important the funeral obsequies seem to the officials of the lodge. During any month except August he conducts religious services of various kinds. He may have more than a few funerals. Does he realize that among the Masons, for instance, the only ceremonies held in public, as a rule, are at a funeral or at the laying of a cornerstone? Is it any wonder that those in charge wish to magnify their offices?

XVII. The Military Funeral

A LOCAL pastor may be invited to take part in a military funeral. Even if he is not, he should be able to advise people who are concerned about the subject. For instance, he should know who may be the officiating clergyman. In the Army the regulations prescribe that the one in charge may be a regular chaplain, that he may be assisted by a civilian clergyman, or that the latter may serve alone. The choice of the minister rests chiefly with the family of the deceased.

The present discussion concerns the Army, with burial by land, not by sea. In the Navy many of the same principles operate. The parish minister is much more likely to take part in a military funeral. What makes a funeral military is the presence of officers and soldiers in a body, showing honor to a fallen comrade, and the carrying out of certain symbolic actions prescribed by the regulations of the Army. Such is the information that has come most graciously from the Office of the Chief of Chaplains at Washington, D. C.

The regulations simply provide for "a decent and orderly way of handling the persons present and of rendering the honors prescribed for the deceased." As for the character and the conduct of the religious services, both elsewhere and at the grave, the regulations are silent. The leader is free. In the prescribed parts of a military funeral, if the clergyman is not a chaplain, he should ask for instructions and then do exactly what he is told by the officer in charge, who is normally the chaplain.

The chaplain in the Army must know many things that do not concern us now. For example, he should be able to serve as the burial officer on the battlefield. If he does so, he must be exceedingly careful about identifying each body, and then marking it for future investigation. He must keep exact and detailed records, far more minute and painstaking than those herein suggested for a parish minister. Years after a hasty burial at night, the chaplain's loving attention to detail may help distraught parents to locate the resting place of their soldier son.

From a study of such regulations any minister can learn the importance of doing the Lord's work decently and in order. Without lack of spirituality or loss of sympathy, the local pastor should be able to do his part in a military funeral with as much skill and precision as the chaplain displays. If any clergyman is unable to qualify, save as a member of an "awkward squad," he should ask to be excused from taking part. Better still, he can learn how to excel in such a Christian ceremony.

According to the regulations, military funerals are of three different kinds. These distinctions are prominent in the literature that guides the Army chaplain. If a civilian clergyman is invited to take part in a military funeral, he should adapt himself to one of the three plans.

The most elaborate procedure is that of the "chapel service." The word "chapel" is interpreted to mean the church, the home, or any other place where funeral services are held, prior to the exercises at the grave. After the chapel service, or, rather, as a vital part, there is a procession to the cemetery, with a military escort. According to this plan, all that is done reaches its climax at the grave.

In the second type of military funeral the procession forms at or near the entrance to the cemetery and marches to the grave. As a rule some kind of religious ceremony has been held previously, perhaps at a distance. In any case it would probably not be military. If it does not seem wise to have military exercises both at the chapel and at the grave, what seems to matter most according to the Army regulations is the service within the cemetery.

The third plan is much more simple. The exercises are only at the grave, with no procession. Since the first type of military funeral really includes the other two, the discussion here relates chiefly to what is known as the "chapel service."

A military procession with full honors affords an awesome spectacle. It consists of the following, in the order prescribed: (1) band, (2) military escort, (3) colors, (4) clergy, (5) caisson or hearse and casket bearers, (6) caparisoned horse (if the deceased had been mounted), (7) honorary pall-bearers, (8) family, (9) patriotic or fraternal organizations, (10) friends.

At the "chapel" the band, the escort, and the colors form in line facing the edifice. The band is on the flank toward which the procession is later to move. Before the bearers remove the casket from the conveyance, the members of the family enter the chapel, followed by their friends. The honorary pallbearers stand at attention, in two ranks, facing each other, so as to form an aisle through which the casket will be borne from the conveyance to the entrance of the chapel.

When all is in readiness the band plays and the procession moves into the chapel. As at a civilian's funeral, the clergyman leads. Within the chapel he does as at other times. He takes his place wherever he is to stand during the service—it may be in the pulpit or at the altar. When everyone is seated and all is hushed he is free to do what his church and his conscience dictate. But woe be to him if he is not prepared to read and speak with a touch of distinction!

After the exercises in the chapel the clergyman leads the procession to the funeral conveyance. There he stands with head uncovered, unless the weather is cold or inclement. When the casket is in place he goes to the front of the caisson or hearse. At the cemetery the clergyman leads the procession to the grave, where he should take his position at the head. After the bearers have deposited the casket on the descending device, they remove from the casket the flag that has been reposing there, and hold it in a horizontal position, waist-high, until the conclusion of taps.

During the procession to the grave the band keeps playing. When all is in readiness for the religious services, the music ceases. Then the clergyman takes charge. He is as free as at any other funeral. If he is wise his words will be few and memorable. After the benediction he moves two steps to the side or the rear so as to make room for the bugler. After the appointed squad has fired three volleys of blank cartridges, the bugler sounds taps.

Thus the military funeral practically comes to an end. The soldiers march from the grave, but no music is prescribed. In fact, there may be a military funeral without a band or certain other features that have been mentioned. In a case where the family of the deceased wish to eliminate nonessentials, all that the regulations of the Army require is the presence of the clergy, the casket bearers, the firing party, and the bugler.

THE RELIGIOUS SERVICES

In planning for his part in a military funeral the clergyman may have difficulty in deciding what to say. Naturally he will follow the customs of his denomination. If they permit a measure of freedom, he may choose between two procedures. The one is more or less military in spirit; the other is not. The one follows the principle of likeness; the other, of contrast. In explaining them both, there is no desire to disparage either. When well done, each is worthy.

According to the first plan, things military enter into practically all that the minister says and does. If the religious exercises consist of nothing more than readings and prayers, they may be about life in terms of Christian warfare, and about death as the warrior's folding up his army tent and the sailing west toward home. This kind of service may call for a poem about facing the last foe without yielding to fear. For instance, take the latter half of Browning's "Prospice." Unfortunately, the words are hard to read well: "I was ever a fighter, so—one fight more."

If there is music, either instrumental or vocal, the spirit may be that of the martial hymn, "The Son of God Goes Forth to War." If the members of the family desire a brief sermon, it may be from one of the many texts that speak about religion and life in terms of Christian warfare. Especially do such passages abound in the writings of Paul. By his use of military and other masculine metaphors he shows how to reach the hearts of stalwart men.

Rom. 13: 12c.	The Armor of Eternal Light.
I Cor. 15: 57.	The Victory of Christ's Warriors.
Eph. 6: 11.	The Armor of God's Soldiers.
I Tim. 6: 12.	The Good Fight of Faith.
II Tim. 2: 3.	The Discipline of God's Soldier.
II Tim. 4: 7, 8.	The Farewell of the Christian Warrior.
Heb. 2: 10.	The Captain of Our Salvation.
Rev. 2: 7.	The Fruits of Christian Conquest.

Such a sermon may well be factual. Here is a case in point. According to *The Christian Century*, April 9, 1941, the father of Martin Niemöller sent the following message through a newspaper correspondent who was returning to the States:

"When you go back to America do not let anyone pity the mother and father of Martin Niemöller. Only pity any follower of Christ who does not know the joy that is set before those who endure the Cross, despising the shame.

"Yes, it is a terrible thing to have a son in a concentration camp. Paula here [the mother] and I know that. But there would be something far more terrible for us: if God had needed a faithful martyr and our Martin had been unwilling."

> " 'Tis man's perdition to be safe,
> When for the truth he ought to die."

In the spirit of Emerson's lines the clergyman may feel led

to stress things military. Again he may be prompted to follow the other plan. Instead of being like what has gone before, and what will follow after, the religious services may stress the love of the Father God and the assurance of the life beyond. In the prayers the minister will remember the soldiers who are present and the cause that they represent. But he will be chiefly concerned about bringing comfort and hope to sorrowing hearts.

Such a service is difficult to plan and still more difficult to carry out. Unless the minister knows how to lead in worship there may seem to be no connection between what he is doing and what the soldiers stand for. In their presence it may require courage for the clergyman to speak out boldly for Christ and the Kingdom. On the other hand, there is nothing that Army men admire more than courage. There is nothing that they need so much as personal friendship with Jesus Christ. Since he is the Saviour and Lord, now and forever, what Christian warrior need fear the worst that death can do?

As a rule this second plan is the procedure that the writer prefers. During the World War I, he ministered to as many soldiers and officers as almost any pastor in the South. Hence he has an abiding concern for the spiritual welfare of Army men. Now that his son and namesake is serving as a chaplain in the Navy, that work is equally dear to his heart.

Any minister who is specially interested should secure the literature recommended below. The small book listed first contains wise suggestions about the leadership of worship among enlisted men of various faiths. There are drawings to make clear the correct procedure at a military or naval funeral.

Informational Readings

Bennett, Chaplain Ivan Loveridge, *Song and Service Book for Ship and Field*. A. S. Barnes & Co., 1941. 75 cents.

The Chief of Infantry, *Basic Field Manual 22-5*. Government Printing Office, Washington, D. C., 1941. Chapter IX. 50 cents.

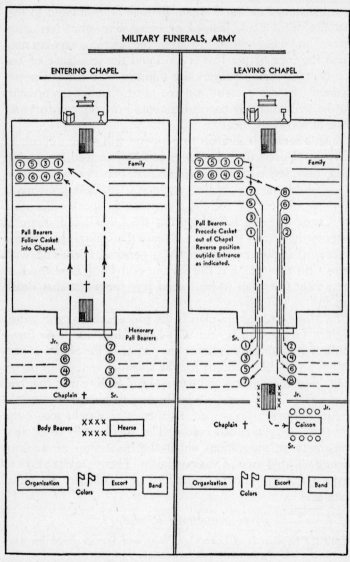

From *The Song and Service Book for Ship and Field*. Edited by Lt. Col.
Ivan L. Bennett. Copyright, 1941, by A. S. Barnes and Company, New
York, New York.

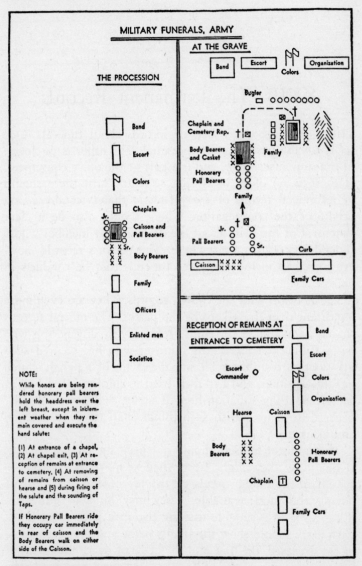

MILITARY FUNERALS, ARMY

AT THE GRAVE

THE PROCESSION

Band

Escort

Colors

Chaplain

Caisson and Pall Bearers

Body Bearers

Family

Officers

Enlisted men

Societies

Bugler

Chaplain and Cemetery Rep.

Body Bearers and Casket

Honorary Pall Bearers

Family

Family

Jr.

Pall Bearers

Sr.

Caisson

Curb

Family Cars

RECEPTION OF REMAINS AT

ENTRANCE TO CEMETERY

Band

Escort

Colors

Organization

Escort Commander

Hearse

Caisson

Body Bearers

Honorary Pall Bearers

Chaplain

Family Cars

NOTE:

While honors are being rendered honorary pall bearers hold the headdress over the left breast, except in inclement weather when they remain covered and execute the hand salute:

(1) At entrance of a chapel, (2) At chapel exit, (3) At reception of remains at entrance to cemetery, (4) At removing of remains from caisson or hearse and (5) during firing of the salute and the sounding of Taps.

If Honorary Pall Bearers ride they occupy car immediately in rear of caisson and the Body Bearers walk on either side of the Caisson.

From *The Song and Service Book for Ship and Field.* Edited by Lt. Col. Ivan L. Bennett. Copyright, 1941, by A. S. Barnes and Company, New York, New York.

XVIII. The Permanent Records

THERE should be two sorts of records about funerals. One set is for the pastor, and is personal. The other is in charge of the church secretary, and is a part of the office equipment. If there is no office or church secretary, still there should be an official record of every funeral that is conducted on behalf of the congregation. There should also be a clear statement of the facts about the death of any member whose funeral has occurred elsewhere. The pastor's records, however, need to include only the funerals that he conducts in person.

Let us begin with the church records. They are even more important than those kept by the pastor. The official records should be available for future reference by any person who has a sufficient reason. Any minister who has secured such information from the sexton or the rector of a parish church in Great Britain, and has then tried to duplicate the feat in a corresponding situation here at home, will determine that henceforth in his parish such things shall be done decently and in order.

The minister himself should not keep the church records. If he did so, they might lapse when he moved away. But he should instill in the minds of the lay officers the ideal of having the facts available. They may be kept either on filing cards in a suitable case or else in a permanent book. Each entry should show the family name and the given name of the deceased, the time and the place of death, the place of burial, the name of the officiating clergyman, and, as a rule, the age of the person at the time of death. These are the facts

that may some time be needed to settle an estate or to complete a genealogical table.

As a rule the church has a weekly calendar or bulletin. If
so, on the Sunday following each funeral there should be
a brief memorial notice concerning the departed. From time
to time the notices should be much the same. Since space
is limited, there need be only a simple heading, such as "In
Loving Memory," "In Memoriam," or "Entered Into Rest."
Immediately below, on three separate lines, carefully centered
and spaced, should appear the name of the deceased, the date
of death, and a few words of Scripture. If the verse is long,
the citation will be sufficient. Occasionally the motto may be
the first line of a hymn.

If the departed friend has been an officer in the church,
or a leader in the women's work, a more extended statement
is fitting. In order to keep from praising one person more
than another, the minister can arrange for the memorial
notice to appear in the name of the board or society concerned. The paragraph in the bulletin need not be long.
The memorial should not be fulsome. But it ought to record
permanently the gratitude of the living for the services
rendered by their former comrade. Incidentally, such notices,
when properly prepared and carefully edited, lend interest
and value to a church bulletin. Often it lacks human warmth
and a spiritual glow.

If there is an office secretary, she should mark on the calendar for the coming year the anniversary date of each
death among the people. When the black day comes round
again, there should go to the family a note of loving sympathy or a bouquet of flowers. Better still, there should be a
call by the minister or some other tactful person.

The carrying out of such a plan calls for thoughtfulness
and care. The marked calendar should be accessible only to
the secretary and the pastor. It should be as complete as
possible. It is better not to single out any such anniversary
than to make much of one and then ignore another. Occa-

sionally there are conditions where any reference to events of a year ago would be embarrassing. In the meantime the vacant place in the home may have been filled by a comely woman who has already heard too much about her angelic predecessor.

In the following case the blackest day of all the year was February 28. Years before, while cleaning his gun, David F. had accidentally killed himself. He had been the only child in a home where the parents were beginning to grow old. Twenty years later, after there had been three changes in the pastorate, a deacon told the new minister that these two friends needed him more on that one day than on any other. While the pastor had never seen the son, there was need that day of a messenger from God. Should not such information be available to each incoming pastor?

PASTORAL RECORDS

The minister also should keep accurate records of each funeral that he conducts. A single card, perhaps four by six inches, affords ample space for all the facts. They are much the same as for the church records. On the pastor's card, however, there should be a record of additional facts that he may wish to recall in later years: for instance, the name of the other minister, the important passages of Scripture, the text and subject of the sermon, the first line of each hymn, and the title of the poem.

Some of these items may go on the other side of the card. In nine cases out of ten the data will never be used. Even so, there can be no harm in having them at hand. If ten years later the minister has to conduct a funeral in the same family circle, he may wish to remember clearly what he said and did the other time.

The cards can be filed either alphabetically or chronologically. In any one pastorate there is an advantage in having the materials arranged according to families, alphabetically. The man who has a shepherd heart thinks of his people by name, not by numbers on the calendar. In later years he will recall each funeral occasion because it concerned human beings whom he loves. When he removes to another field he will set all these records off by themselves, and then make a new start. But there should be no private bonfire.

At first a man shrinks from such clerical detail. Even if there is a church secretary or two, the pastor needs to supply some of the data. He must also supervise the keeping of the records. As time goes on, the number of funerals will increase. If the pastor thinks he is too busy to keep records, he should call on a friendly physician and ask how he keeps countless items accurately. The doctor can immediately bring out from his files a card showing the facts about any case, past or present. Should not the physician of souls be equally careful?

LEGAL PROBLEMS

Occasionally the pastor must appear in court to testify as a witness. In the presence of a judge and other attorneys, as well as a jury, all of whom attach importance to precise records, the clergyman may have to testify that he ministered at a certain deathbed or in the funeral service. He need never divulge what he has learned in confidence—unless by keeping silent he would violate the laws of God and man. But he should be able to produce the exact data, and provide the requisite proofs.

Such legal problems seldom arise. Nevertheless, the pastor should be informed about the laws of the commonwealth where he resides. (Such information is even more vital in the case of marriages than with reference to funerals.) The following statement has been prepared with the help of Robert B. Knowles, Esq., who for years has been a ruling elder in Central Presbyterian Church, Summit, New Jersey. He is a prominent member of the bar in New York City. He assumes that the laws of that commonwealth are typical of such statutes elsewhere.

1. The Public Health Law regulates and controls the duties and responsibilities of those who have to do with births and deaths. Such control includes the physician, the surgeon, the nurse, the mortician, and the clergyman.

2. A physician licensed by the state and duly registered must issue a death certificate, which must be filed with the authorized city or state official. The filing is done by the mortician. He must be registered by the state as an embalmer.

3. The authorized city or state official then issues to the registered embalmer a permit for burial, cremation, or removal to another state. In Massachusetts the state laws require that a body be embalmed before it can be cremated.

4. In the case of a suicide, a death by accident, or when there is a suspicion of foul play, the city or state officials have the right to withhold the permit for burial until the matter has been investigated to their satisfaction. The procedure may include a post-mortem, as well as an inquest under the coroner, who may or may not summon a jury.

5. After the proper authorities have issued the permit for burial or cremation, the mortician and the minister may proceed with plans for the funeral.

These are the facts, legally. Within his own parish, and often elsewhere, the minister can ignore them all. But he should be careful to keep his records straight. He should exercise caution in dealing with strangers. For example, if the body is cremated, it is vital that all the legal formalities be observed. If the minister knows and trusts the mortician, there is little need for anything more than accurate records. But some day, if the man of God is concerned exclusively about things beyond the clouds, he may wish that he had kept his feet on the ground.

The following case was unique. In it no one was to blame. In a capital city a minister conducted the services over the body of a derelict found floating in the river. Before the interment there had been a careful investigation. A few weeks later the clergyman received a visit from an aged widow who lived in a distant part of the state. She brought a letter from her pastor, who joined with her in the plea that the body be disinterred. The widow and her minister felt certain that it was the body of her son.

The local pastor was a busy man. But his heart went out to the widow. He learned that her son had been a lifelong imbecile. He had been confined in the state hospital, from which he had escaped. The mother wished to know whether he was dead, or was wandering helpless among strangers, some of whom might be cruel. She knew that the hospital authorities had measured the derelict's body with care. They insisted that it could not be her son. Nevertheless, she was importunate. By persistence she and the minister gained permission to have the body exhumed.

At length, to the satisfaction of all concerned, she established her son's identity. Despite the fact that the body taken out of the river had been six inches longer than the person whom the attendants at the hospital had measured, there could be no doubt concerning the identity. The superintendent acknowledged that he and his staff had been mistaken. He supposed that the body must have swollen while in the river. The minister suspected that some careless attendant had guessed at the height and missed it by six inches.

To that one case, involving complete strangers, the pastor devoted much of his time for two days. In the end he had the satisfaction of bringing peace to a troubled mother's heart. He had likewise learned much about legal technicalities and still more about human fallibilities. In after days he wondered if he would have been willing to have some of his other funerals investigated by the legal and medical authorities of the city where he was a pastor. To the best of his knowledge he had never officiated at services where he was helping to conceal a crime. But he could visualize such a possibility.

The minister concerned does not object to cremation. But he has often wondered how that widow could have found peace if her son's body had been burned. The obvious inference is that the authorities should be able to disinter the remains of any person about whose death there can ever be any question. A more personal consideration is that no legal inquiry ought to involve the fair name of the minister who conducts the funeral. If he must come into court, he should have clean hands and a calm heart. The heart will be more peaceful if the hands are holding adequate records.

Informative Readings

Brand, N. F., and Ingram, V. M., *The Pastor's Legal Adviser.* Abingdon-Cokesbury, 1942.

XIX. The Rising Costs

SOME of the most perplexing problems relating to funerals
have to do with the rising costs. In modern parlance the subject of this chapter would be "The High Cost of Dying."
Unfortunately, there seems to be little that the minister can
do. His hands appear to be tied. As a rule he has no share
in making funeral arrangements that require money. With
minor exceptions, he seems powerless to change local customs, however pagan. Nevertheless, he should be aware of
what often goes on behind the scenes.

The costs come all in a heap. After a protracted illness,
which has drained the household treasury, there is need of
money for the purchase of the burial plot or the niche in the
columbarium; the digging of the grave; the purchase of the
casket (this item usually includes other professional services); the buying of wearing apparel for the body and
mourning garments for the widow as well as for other members of the family. Then there may be the expense of securing
carriages for relatives and friends. Later will come the bill
for the headstone or other marker at the grave.

The list is not complete. It makes no mention of the
flowers purchased by sympathetic friends or of such items as
telegrams and long-distance calls, and the entertainment of
guests from a distance. In one case a Negro family in Ala-
bama shipped the body of the deceased father to Pennsylvania and back. Thereby they escaped the expenses incident
to a gala funeral at home. Even so, those simple-minded folk
probably fell victims to some undertaker like the one who
advertised the following rates for professional services:

"For composing the features, $1.00.
"For giving the appearance of quiet resignation, $2.00.
"For giving the appearance of Christian hope, $5.00."

Prior to the collapse of the boom in 1929, "the high cost of dying" had become so notorious that there were various investigations. The findings were disconcerting. One research specialist discovered that certain undertakers were charging the patron six times the original cost of the casket. The calculation did not include the cost of professional services. Those the statistical expert computed separately.

THE MORTICIAN

There is much to be said for conscientious morticians. Those whom the writer has known best have been high-minded Christian gentlemen. In his last congregation there were two, representing different firms, each of which had a code of honor. On the other hand, there were in the city a few undertakers on a level with quacks among doctors and ambulance chasers among lawyers. As a rule shysters and tricksters do not belong to a reputable association, such as "The National Selected Morticians."

Such a businessman faces a financial problem. His income is intermittent. In summer funerals may be few. In late winter, when his work is most difficult and costly, there may be many deaths. In an establishment of any size there may be several funerals at the same hour of the afternoon. In summer as well as winter the equipment and the staff must be ready for an emergency. For all this someone must pay.

The overhead is high. The annual budget must provide for the equipment and maintenance of funeral parlors, costly conveyances, a number of drivers, and a staff of experts, one of whom must be a licensed embalmer. There are also expenses for clerical help, and many other items. Even if every bill were paid at once and in full, the financing of the concern might not be easy. From year to year the expense of doing business has kept rising.

From the mortician's point of view the secret of keeping down the costs lies in co-operation among competitors. From the minister's standpoint the question concerns the friends who must meet the funeral expenses, often unexpectedly. With unpaid bills from the physician and the surgeon, the hospital and the nurses, the druggist and the grocer, the person in charge at the home must face a number of other accounts, some of which call for cash. Meanwhile the household expenses may have doubled, temporarily, and the income may have stopped, permanently.

In another home the conditions are quite the reverse. There is a lot of new money. Sometimes the situation is complicated by the life insurance agent. As a rule he too is a Christian gentleman, but when he is not, there may be an awkward situation. As far back as 1905 abuses among industrial life insurance agents had become so glaring that the chief company in the field, the Metropolitan, forbade any of its agents to have business dealings with an undertaker. The company also urged every agent to warn the patron against incurring needless expenses for the funeral. Unfortunately, such counsel is usually wasted. Local custom prevails. It leads to extravagance.

Think of a case, which is not unique. The widow has had no experience in handling large sums of money. At times she has felt that too much of the family income has been going into life insurance and not enough into making the home happy. Soon after her husband's death she discovers that she has at her disposal thousands of dollars, where she has been thinking in terms of dimes.

In the hour of grief the widow is surrounded by sobbing friends who tell her that nothing is too good for the funeral of her dear husband, and that she must keep up with the standards of other people who live down the street.

Into this milieu comes the mortician. He also is human. He feels sure that the money will soon be scattered. He is not averse to a funeral that will compare with the work of his competitors. In short, while neither the widow nor the mortician may be consciously at fault, the funeral is likely to help to negative the plans of the deceased for the future comfort of his family.

THE PASTOR

A little later the pastor confers with the widow about the approaching services. He brings her the Gospel of comfort and hope. He is thinking about the world to come, not about funeral costs. He may wonder why he finds it difficult to keep his friend's attention fixed on the things that are unseen and eternal. If he becomes aware of the struggle between God and Mammon, he may wonder if there is not something he can do to stress laying up treasures in heaven.

It is not easy to deal with such a situation. Theoretically, it should be possible for a pastor to train his people so that they will use all their money for the glory of the God from whom it comes. Practically, it is hard to promote trusteeship at any time, and doubly so when there is a death in the home.

The subject of trusteeship is too large for us to consider now. In the case just mentioned the wife should long since have had a share in the larger concerns of household finance. The basic need here is justice. There is also a place for the use of money as an expression of love. What else did the Lord Jesus have in view when he commended Mary for her lavish gift of ointment? "She did it for my burial. Verily I say unto you, Wheresoever this gospel shall be preached in the whole world, there shall also this, that this woman hath done, be told for a memorial of her" (Matt. 26: 12, 13).

On the other hand, it is hard to invoke the blessing of God on the pagan display that marks many a funeral. For instance, think of the flowers. Somewhere between niggardliness and prodigality there is a Christian way of showing love for the one who has fallen asleep. In as far as the minister has any influence he will exert it in the promotion of simplicity.

He will foster the feeling that the funeral service should call no attention to itself, but turn every eye toward God.

It is almost never wise for the pastor to mention "the high cost of dying." No matter what the occasion, he is likely to be misunderstood. Unintentionally, he may hurt the feelings of a mortician or a florist who does his best to prevent extravagant display. There may also seem to be a criticism of church members who were responsible for a funeral months before. After a few futile attempts to change non-Christian customs, the minister will probably decide that he must leave the whole problem to his successor.

A concrete case will show part of the difficulty. In California a public-school teacher learned by telegraph that an aunt had died back in Virginia. While he scarcely knew her, he sent word that she should be properly interred at his expense. In a few weeks he received a bill for $400, which represented his salary for two months. At the same time, in 1940, the United States Army regulations for the funeral of a soldier read in part as follows:

"Burial expenses proper are restricted to undertaker's services, cost of casket, cost of outside box or shipping case, and hire of hearse. The general limitation on these expenses is $85. The amount may be extended to $100 on authority of the quartermaster general." After having had more or less to do with military funerals, the writer can testify that the financial provision has always seemed adequate.

THE FUNERAL FEE

One thing the minister can do from the very first day in the parish. He can refrain from exacting payment for his own services. Among the members of the congregation he may decline to receive compensation for anything that he does in the presence of death. If some of his people have abundant means, and if they insist on his receiving a token of their gratitude, he can take their gift with thanks. If it is money, he can apply it to some part of the church work. In that event he may ask the treasurer or the church secretary to write the donors a letter of thanks.

In dealing with persons who were not as yet affiliated with the local church the writer adopted much the same procedure. Year after year the funeral fees were larger than those at weddings. The latter went to the mistress of the manse; the former, into the treasury of the church or of some society. Whenever he was offered a funeral fee, the pastor explained that there was no charge. But if the people insisted on paying, and if they were able to do so without hardship, the minister felt that it was a kindness to let them aid in supporting the church. Thus the use of money may be a means of grace.

Throughout the community the pastor should become known as a neighbor and friend upon whom any person can call for ministerial services that are absolutely free. His time and strength belong to Christ and the home church. If an exceptional case arises, when he does not know whether or not to receive money on behalf of the congregation, he ought to solve the problem in the light of a golden text. One of many is the key verse in the Gospel of service:

"The Son of man came not to be ministered unto, but to minister, and to give his life a ransom for many" (Mark 10: 45).

Informational Readings

Dowd, Quincy Lamartine, *Funeral Management and Costs.* The University of Chicago Press, 1921.

Gebhart, John Charles, *Funeral Costs.* G. P. Putnam's Sons, 1928. Report of an investigation under a committee appointed by the Metropolitan Life Insurance Company.

XX. The Funeral Code

THE heading above represents an ideal. There is in print no official code of honor to guide a young Protestant clergyman with reference to funerals or to any other part of his pastoral work. While certain branches of the Church have drawn up ethical codes, no one of them has any binding force. As a rule they are general, and do not touch the funeral. Hence it is the part of wisdom for each minister to formulate his own personal code, which may not be in writing. It should include such items as the following:

1. The Christian minister is the servant of the community, not merely of his parish.

2. The physician of souls responds at once to the call from a dying man, whether he is a friend or a stranger.

3. The ministering shepherd goes at once to the home where there has been a death.

4. The Christian minister carries out these principles in the spirit of the Golden Rule. It forbids the stealing of sheep.

5. The pastor is directly responsible for the spiritual ministry at any deathbed or funeral service in his congregation.

6. The Golden Rule leads any minister to confer with the pastor before rendering any service in the other man's parish.

7. The former pastor accepts such an invitation, if at all, only when it comes through the present minister.

8. In an emergency the Christian clergyman responds to the call of human need and afterward makes his peace with any other minister concerned.

9. The Christian clergyman never submits a bill for services rendered, and never indirectly solicits payment. How-

ever, he is entitled to receive money sufficient to defray his traveling expenses.

10. The pastor holds inviolate everything that he learns in confidence, notably a deathbed confession.

PRACTICAL SUGGESTIONS

1. Be patient. In the time of critical illness or sudden sorrow the shortcomings of human nature are likely to be intensified. People who are in suspense, or else all let down, may say and do strange things. They sometimes make impossible demands. Whatever the provocation, the minister of Christ should control his temper, keep his poise, and hold his tongue. The secret of doing so is to pray.

2. Remember that the mortician is in charge of the preliminary arrangements and the public services. He has practically nothing to do with the religious exercises, but he is responsible for everything else. The wise minister is glad to be released from concern about business arrangements and practical details. If things go awry he should not interfere, even to proffer advice. As in dealing with a physician, the clergyman keeps to his own field. However, when the mortician does an excellent piece of work, a note of appreciation from the minister is a kindness.

3. In public as in private treat the mortician as an equal. He too has his professional honor. Do not refer to him as an "undertaker." When you first enter a parish become acquainted with the reputable morticians. If a certain family is in financial straits, suggest to the deacons that they confer with the mortician in charge about extending the time for payment. He may even reduce his bill, especially if the deacons are willing to help him to defray the actual costs. In short, treat the mortician as a human being with a heart. Erelong he should become a personal friend.

4. When in doubt concerning a matter beyond the congregation, it may be wise to consult with the mortician. Here is a case in point. Two young men requested a Protestant

clergyman to officiate at the funeral of their mother. From birth she had been a Catholic, but she was not in good standing with her priest. Because she had been attending another Roman church, and had not kept up her pew rents, he refused to perform the burial rites.

The Protestant minister was young and inexperienced. He wished to help the young men but he was dubious about conducting services in a Catholic home and cemetery. He thanked the young men for coming, assured them of his desire to do all he could, and suggested that they talk things over with the mortician in charge.

A few days afterward the clergyman asked the mortician what had taken place. The latter replied: "I told the young men that there would be hard feelings if you buried their mother in holy ground. Since they much preferred a Catholic funeral I offered to intercede for them with the German priest. I took them to his home, where I held a private interview with him. He protested that the woman had been untrue to her parish church. I agreed with him but I pleaded for leniency. At last, grudgingly, he said: 'Tell the boys to bring the old woman to the church tomorrow for eight o'clock mass. If they hand me ten dollars, the matter will be closed.' " Both the mortician and the minister knew that no other priest in that part of the city would have been so heartless.

5. A much more timely suggestion relates to the presence of a second clergyman. As a rule the practice should be discouraged. Especially in a brief service, a single leader is almost always preferable to more than one. On the other hand, the pastor cannot ignore the desire of the family that there be another minister or two. The pastor should extend the invitation heartily, and any brother who accepts should feel sure that he is welcome.

6. When two ministers are conducting a service, the home pastor should be in charge. He should make the plans. He himself should take the opening part. He should ask the

other minister to do whatever the friends desire. In any case, each man should be brief, and confine himself strictly to what has been agreed upon in private conference. For instance, it is embarrassing if the one who utters the opening words of prayer does all that the other one plans to do later in the service. Here again, follow the Golden Rule.

7. When a minister relinquishes a pastoral charge, he relinquishes the privileges as well as the responsibilities. As soon as his successor enters the field, the former minister should give the other man the right of way. Especially during the first year or two of the new regime, the part of kindness is not to accept invitations to assist at funerals in the former parish. Of course there may be exceptions. In each case the determining factor should be the advancement of the Kingdom in the congregation that both the ministers love.

8. A still more personal warning relates to professionalism. It manifests itself whenever a minister can look on death with heart unmoved, and whenever he can conduct a funeral without the expenditure of nervous energy. At such a time self-control and a gift of leadership are sorry substitutes for spirituality and sympathy. Especially in a day when the world is at war, the heart of a Christian minister ought to be full of love.

Professionalism may also lead the clergyman to relate amusing incidents about a deathbed scene or funeral service. In fact, there has often been a temptation to do so in this book. Blessed is the pastor or physician to whom God has given a saving sense of humor. But neither of them ought ever to tell a joke about death and the grave. Like Phillips Brooks, the clergyman today should be a lover of fun, but not a clerical jester. In brief, let the clergyman be a clergyman.

9. The best time to prepare the people of God for sickness and sorrow is while they are well and strong. That is when their spiritual mentor should interpret the Ninetieth

Psalm and other Biblical teachings about time and eternity, the great white throne, and the Judgment Day. "The wages of sin is death; but the gift of God is eternal life." "Watch therefore, for ye know neither the day nor the hour wherein the Son of man cometh." Whenever he appears, be ready to meet him with joy and to serve him in glory. Such are the teachings of the good pastor.

10. Much the same principles apply to the preparation by the minister. The time to make ready for usefulness at a deathbed or in a funeral service is long before the call has come. If it were necessary for people in sorrow to choose—as it is not—between the prepared heart without an orderly program and the orderly program without the prepared heart, they would prefer the man whose heart is right with God.

Informational Readings

Harmon, Nolan Bailey, Jr., *Ministerial Ethics and Etiquette*. The Cokesbury Press, 1928 (bibliography).

Jefferson, Charles Edward, *Building of the Church*. The Macmillan Company, 1910.

Post, Emily Price, *Etiquette*. Funk & Wagnalls Company, 1937 (25th Edition).

XXI. The Problem Funeral

A CERTAIN funeral may cause the pastor more concern than a dozen others. In such an event books may be of little help. Naturally, they deal with the dozen cases that are normal rather than the one that is unique. In our work, as in medicine, facts have a way of defying theories. Under the guidance of the Holy Spirit, therefore, the minister has to work out his own salvation. Often there may be fear and trembling.

If a man trusts God, and works hard, he will find out what to do and say at each problem funeral. Fortunately, such occasions are likely to come seldom, and at intervals. Instead of discussing the problems abstractly, let us look at a number of actual cases. The principles that emerge should prove helpful in deciding on a course of action amid still other circumstances. The main thing, on the human level, is to sympathize. Even when one of the bereaved cries out, "My God, my God, why?" the minister should know how to "trace the rainbow through the rain."

A SUICIDE

John Doe, forty years of age, was highly esteemed. He was the cashier of a prominent bank and the treasurer of his church. One day, without warning anyone, he shot himself and died instantly. When the authorities investigated, they discovered that he had been gambling on the stock market. He had appropriated large sums from the bank and had used up the small vested holdings of his church. Doubtless he knew that the facts were about to be revealed. Hence he took what the man of the world styles "the easy way out." Out to what?

From this point onward the statements are hypothetical. While the minister is hastening to the home he is wondering what he can say. He has never had occasion to question the integrity and honor of the deceased. Much as the pastor knows that the congregation will feel the financial loss, far more does he dread the spiritual effect on the family and the community. Once again, as with Judas, a strong man has given way to the lure of silver. But still the pastor should not judge or condemn.

The first thing he does is to pray. Long since he should have learned that it is possible to do so while hastening to the home of sorrow. If he goes in faith, as the servant of the Lord, the Spirit will guide. At such a time the rule is, "A minister has no more religion than he displays in an emergency."

Within the home the pastor expresses his sympathy. At first he may have little or nothing to say about the facts in the case or about the departed. Probably everyone is too distracted for coherent thinking. If the minister makes any remark, however harmless, he may be misunderstood. At such a tragic hour he should be careful about the neighborhood purveyor of gossip, as well as the ever-present reporter.

If the household is in turmoil, the presence of one man who is calm may serve as a spiritual stabilizer. As soon as the pastor can do so, he arranges to talk alone with the widow, or some other person who ought to be in charge. Speaking for the sake of the family, he may advise that the funeral services and the interment be private. If he does not know the people well enough to proffer advice, he may get in touch with the mortician, directly or by telephone, and ask him to make the suggestion. Any such conversation should be strictly confidential.

At first the widow is likely to be overcome. She may be under the care of a physician, who has to administer a sedative. But sooner or later there will be an opportunity for her to talk at length with the pastor. If he is comparatively a stranger, she may send for his predecessor, or some neighboring clergyman. With her may be the daughter, and perhaps other members of the family circle.

As a rule it is wise to let the widow, or it may be the oldest son, keep on talking until there is nothing more to be said. Like Job's wife in her extremity, the widow's words may be wild and bitter. Justly or unjustly, she may reproach her husband. Perhaps mistakenly, on the other hand, she may feel that she herself has been chiefly at fault. It may be that both have had wrong attitudes toward money and toward God. Fortunately, the pastor is not their judge. He commits all these matters to the only One who knows; that is the Lord.

After the widow has exhausted herself, and everyone has become silent, the pastor should speak. Perhaps the kindest thing to say is this: "Your husband was my friend. So are you. Let us both remember about him all the good that we can recall. At the last he probably was not himself. He must have worried so long over his wrongdoings that temporarily he lost control of himself."

Gradually the pastor can encourage the widow to forgive the most tragic injustice that she has ever endured. He may succeed in persuading her to recall whatsoever things have been true and pure and beautiful in the life of the deceased. Even if the pastor feels certain that the banker stole in order to meet increasingly exorbitant demands from his wife and grown children, the hour has come for Christian mercy. If there ought to be a sterner note about justice, in due time the conscience will speak.

In the funeral services, whether they be private or public, there should be no allusion to suicide. It would not be hard to read up about Judas, or King Saul, and then consult *The Pilgrim's Progress*, where Bunyan discusses Doubting Castle and Giant Despair. From Bedford Jail come ten reasons why a man should not be guilty of self-murder.

To the sensationalist the facts would suggest a lurid discourse. But the heart of a pastor revolts against any suggestion that he make capital out of human sorrow. The circumstances call for a brief service of Christian comfort. Fortunately, at other times he has led his people not to expect a funeral eulogy. He may have established the reputation of doing nothing more than read from the Bible and then pray to God. If so, he brings the family to the foot of the Cross, and leaves them there, close to the heart of the heavenly Father.

After the funeral there is much for the pastor to do. Gradually, in the home, or perhaps in his study, he can guide the widow as she makes her readjustments, spiritually. Indirectly, he can see that the most winsome and tactful women of the parish go out of their way to show their sister in Christ friendship and esteem. Instead of treating her as a social outcast, and thus permitting her to develop an inferiority complex, he and the others can make it clear that the congregation is a household of faith, and that God's children never desert a loved one in need of Christian sympathy.

A STREET FATALITY

James X, twelve years of age, was a communicant member of the church, which he had recently joined through confession and baptism. His parents were adherents. While riding on his bicycle at dusk he was struck by an automobile. Soon afterward he died. The driver of the car was eighteen years of age, and a member of the same congregation; so were his parents. A few weeks later at the trial the young man narrowly escaped being convicted of manslaughter. A deacon in the home church testified that he had been an eyewitness and that the young man had been blameless.

On the part of the little boy's parents and friends there

was bitterness. They felt aggrieved at the church to which
both the driver and the chief witness belonged. On the side
of the young man there was bewilderment. The father, who
was an invalid, made generous financial arrangements with
the people who were bereaved, and did everything in his
power to show them sympathy. But the young man's relatives felt that he could not have avoided hitting the boy,
who had been riding on the wrong side of the street, and
with no lights on his wheel.

To the theorist, who concerns himself only with supernal
mysteries, these details may seem inconsequential. But to the
pastor of a neighborhood church, life is made up largely of
relations among people who are far from perfect. In that
prolonged dispute the pastor took no part. He admired the
restraint of the young man's relatives and he shared with
everyone in sympathy for the victims of a mechanized "civi-
lization." In vain the minister strove to have the differ-
ences settled out of court. To no avail he pleaded with the
boy's parents to be reconciled to the young man's people.

In this case, as in a number of other problem funerals,
the pastor felt that he had partially failed. As a rule the
books for ministers record only the writers' successes. But
candor compels any pastor to confess that his attainments
often fall below his ideals. His failures ought to keep him
humble. They should likewise lead him to consult with
other ministers so as to learn from their experiences how to
meet trying situations. From the medical fraternity we
should learn the value of frequent consultations with masters in the same profession.

As for the funeral services, they were held in the boy's
home. Because of the newspaper publicity, there was a
throng of curiosity seekers. Everyone wondered what the
minister would say. To the disappointment of many, he did
not allude to the tragedy. Rather did he stress the fact that
the Father God knows how to make heaven seem like home
to a growing boy, and how to bring forth all "the full-grown

energies that suit the purposes of heaven." Whether or not
that kind of comfort was what the family desired he never
felt sure. At least he held their friendship and he made them
aware of God's unfailing love.

A PROFLIGATE

Samuel M. was sixty-five years of age. He was accounted
the most wicked man in his part of the city. He had been
guilty of almost every sin except murder. While he was
dying with pneumonia the woman in attendance was his
latest paramour. Years before, by cruelty and abuse, he had
caused his wife to seek refuge elsewhere, and he had helped
to break the hearts of other women. In short, if in the other
world there were no place for such a person, there would
need to be some extra provision. At least he was not consciously a candidate for heaven.

Somewhere in the entourage, however, there was a vestige
of religion. When the neighboring pastor was called in, he
found in the dying man no evidence of repentance or remorse
for broken vows, bruised hearts, blasted hopes. Each evening
he called but apparently without avail. The dying man seemed
to appreciate the presence of the clergyman and to be willing
for prayer, or anything else. But in as far as the minister
could see, there was no change in the heart of the sinner.
He died as he had lived, without God.

In that community everyone expected a funeral sermon.
For a while the minister was at a loss about what to say. At
last he recalled a conversation with the woman of the
ménage. She had told him that the deceased was passionately
fond of flowers. At heart a man of that type is often a lover
of beauty. This may be partly why he can appeal to women.
Much as they have to endure at his hands, they respond to
his quest for beauty.

In the services the clergyman read the Ninetieth Psalm. A
little later he spoke about the God of the flowers (Ps. 103:
15). In the most beautiful of all the psalms the stress is on

the loving-kindness of the Father God. In the heart of the song there is a strain about the frailties of man.

At such a time the man of God wonders why there should be a funeral sermon. When his heart has its way, there need be nothing more than the reading of Biblical passages and prayers that he finds in his favorite book of forms. At first glance such a procedure may seem unsympathetic, or even cowardly. But this is a wise rule: when there is nothing good to say, say nothing specific.

A more delicate case was that of Susan N. She was thirty-five years of age, and presumably a widow. Because of her sins, she was dying with tuberculosis. Before her final illness she had been comely. She had appealed especially to men. In the neighborhood for years she had been known as a prostitute.

Perhaps because of her childhood training, she was much concerned about religion. After she was confined to her bed she sent for the same minister as in the case just reported. Again and again he called, but never when he would be alone with the dying woman. Always he found her responsive to his readings and his prayers, as well as his words about the way back to God. But never could he note any sign of penitence and change of heart.

After she died the clergyman was asked to officiate at the services in the home. In that back street any funeral was a neighborhood event. This time the little house was sure to be filled to overflowing. Everyone wondered what the parson would say. So did he for he was young. Never before in his life, to his knowledge, had he spoken to a prostitute.

Sitting in his study he was thinking about what he had learned of the woman's childhood in a Christian home. Then he looked out upon the snow that covered the earth and made even the city slums look white and clean. In the gospel of the snow he found a message from the heart of God (Isa. 1: 18; Ps. 51: 7b; or Isa. 55: 10, 11). While he did not use the poem in the services, he read to himself more than

once from Palgrave's *Golden Treasury* the familiar words of
Thomas Hood in "The Bridge of Sighs." This is a brief
portion:

> "Touch her not scornfully,
> Think of her mournfully,
> Gently and humanly;
> Not of the stains of her—
> All that remains of her
> Now is pure womanly."

On the way to the cemetery the pastor rode with the only
two relatives who were present. These brothers had come
from a neighboring city, where they had left their aged
parents, broken in heart. With eyes full of tears the brothers
thanked the minister for his sympathy and his message. They
explained that even in girlhood their sister had resisted the
efforts of her godly mother and father to keep her from
going astray. In every sense she had seemed to be a prodigal
daughter, except that she never repented.

The brothers were Christian men, and active in the home
church. They were glad that the minister had held high the
standards of the Christian faith, and that he had not spoken
directly about their sister. They loved to think that she might
have repented ere she fell asleep, and thus fulfilled the vows
with which she had long since been dedicated to the Lord.
They said that as long as they lived they would think of God
and his redeeming grace whenever they looked out on the
sermon in the snow.

A YOUNG CRIMINAL

The following case is perhaps the most perplexing of all.
John R. was twenty-two years of age. He had been reared in
a humble home where both his parents feared the Lord and
loved the Church. Early in life he had broken loose, partly
because they were of foreign birth and speech. He had gone
from bad to worse and had become a professional criminal.
One night he took a leading part in the robbery of a bank.

A few days afterward he was arrested for the murder of the night watchman.

During the trial, which was speedy, the parents attended daily. They heard the judge pronounce the final sentence and they watched their son walk out toward the death chamber. Then they went back to their home. Meanwhile the penitentiary chaplain had striven to comfort them, and had promised to deal with their son on behalf of Christ. But all that minister's efforts seemed to be fruitless. The young man went to his death as he had gone through life, defying God.

At the home town of the parents, in a distant part of the state, the pastor was new on the field. He had never seen the son, and knew of him only through the newspapers and also through the parents. When the minister learned that the young man had been condemned to die, the man of God did his best to prepare the mother and father for the oncoming shock. The pastor suggested that the funeral services be private. Even so, he wondered what he should say to those childlike people.

On the afternoon when the parents were at the railroad station waiting for the train that was to bring home the body of their son, the pastor was by their side. Since he did not know what to say, he kept silent. In later years he has often wondered what he could have said or done to show his sympathy and faith in God.

To such a question, there may be no answer, at least on the human level. According to the *British Weekly*, during the first World War a Christian widow was watering her roses one morning while she was praying for her soldier son, the only child, who was in the front-line trenches across the Channel. She loved to think of him as the living image of the young father whom he had never seen.

Then she saw a lad coming up the hill on his bicycle with a telegram. When she opened the envelope, she learned that her son had been slain in battle. Seeing that the mes-

senger was waiting for a reply, she said to him softly, "There
is no answer."

But that is not the last word. It must come from God.
Silent sympathy has its place. When the time comes for his
servant to speak, the words may be few and faltering. Even
so, they should have to do with the compassion of God:
"Like as a father pitieth his children, so the Lord pitieth
them that fear him" (Ps. 103: 13). "As one whom his
mother comforteth, so will I comfort you" (Isa. 66: 13).

While passing these cases in review, almost every minister
is sure to recall others equally perplexing. Whatever the circumstances and the difficulties, one fact is clear: the pastor
should respond immediately to any such call for his services.
Not to do so might come close to the unpardonable sin. In
the autobiography of George A. Gordon, *My Education and
Religion,* is the account of an experience that must have been
without a parallel:

"A man of very bad repute had died, and the Episcopalian,
Presbyterian, Methodist, Baptist, and Congregationalist ministers declined to officiate at the funeral, on account of previous engagements. The only minister available was the Uni-
tarian. The widow of the deceased refused to let him conduct
the service, declaring with warmth of feeling, 'No minister
is fit to conduct that service who does not believe in hell!' "

What the widow had in mind no one can say. But surely it
should not have been necessary for her to go shopping round
for a clergyman who was willing to assure her that God
cared for her soul. In the funeral of a man whose life has
been wholly evil, the services are for the sake of those who
survive. Whatever the circumstances, the minister of Christ
should respond, and that willingly.

In the service there need be no allusion to the departed,
or to the facts in the case. If the exercises must be in public,
the clergyman can read from his favorite book of forms. The
fact that the Scripture passages and the prayers are somewhat
general makes them all the more suitable for a problem

funeral. If a man has a shepherd heart, he will also utter
petitions of his own. All the while he will deal tenderly
with those that are bruised.

"THE GOOD MORAL MAN"

Much the same principles apply when the deceased has
been indifferent to religion, rather than depraved in morals.
At the funeral the clergyman is likely to swing to one or the
other of two extremes. If he is a "jolly good fellow," he may
give the impression that it makes little difference whether
or not a person had been loyal to Christ and His Church. On
the other hand, if the pastor prides himself on his Puritanism,
he may seem to be standing in judgment where God alone
has a right to speak. What, then, shall the minister say?

At a county seat in North Jersey a young pastor reports
that half of his funerals are in circles with no semblance of
religion. For instance, the head of the household may have
had a vague conception of a "grandmotherly God." The man
may have held a churchless creed about being a jolly good
fellow. He may have boasted, "I get my religion from the
Sermon on the Mount," by which he meant a mild humani-
tarianism. When death has struck him down custom calls for
a funeral service to be in charge of a Protestant clergyman
who is sure to be "safe." There may even be a request for a
sermon.

Amid such surroundings two things are clear, negatively.
One is, do not discuss ethics. Another is, do not deal with
eschatology. What, then, is left? The basic truth about God!
If the deceased has been a husband and father, that may be a
good place to begin. The text may be from the Sermon on the
Mount, and from The Lord's Prayer, "Our Father." Since
there is time to make clear and luminous only a single truth,
let it be about God as Father. That is the bedrock in our
religion. Everyone present at the funeral needs to know God
and love him as Father.

If such a line of thought raises more questions than it

answers, is it not good for worldly folk to start thinking about God? As for the answers to their questions, there should be more than one quiet personal conference soon after the funeral obsequies. The physician of souls almost never does his most effective work in public and en masse.

Whatever the immediate facts, it is possible for the Christian clergyman to speak out for God. Let him do it boldly, and yet kindly. On the human level there may be little that he can say without being misunderstood. But why should the man who represents God in the community have to tarry long on the human level? Without being a disciple of Karl Barth, any minister should agree with the most famous words from that master of paradox:

"As ministers we ought to speak of God. We are human, however, and so cannot speak of God. We ought therefore to recognize both our obligation and our inability, and by that very recognition give God the glory. This is our perplexity. The rest of our task fades into insignificance in comparison."

Let no one think of such positive preaching as an evasion, or defense mechanism. After all, God alone can change the hearts of those who hear a funeral message. His Word shall not return unto him void. After a funeral service in the far Middle West, when the deceased had been a pronounced unbeliever, but never known as a "bad" man, the pastor was able to lead into the fellowship of Christ and the home church the various members of the household, every one of whom had hitherto been devoid of religion.

In the services over an unbeliever it is possible to make God seem so real, and Christ so precious, that some of those assembled will long to know God better and love him more. Erelong, under wise pastoral leadership, such persons should find their way to the foot of the cross. The evangelistic appeal, however, should come in private, not in public. Evidently, there is no cheap and easy way for a minister to do his duty at the funeral of a "good moral man."

Another word of caution is needful. Only God knows the

facts about the deceased. He may have been living a double life. Fortunately, the clergyman is not the judge. But neither is he the advocate. Every word that he utters should be true in the sight of God. The call is not merely for good intentions and veracity. A man must be certain about any facts to which he refers. For instance, at the obsequies of a widow who had supported her household by living in adultery, the visiting clergyman prayed that the two growing daughters might follow in their mother's footsteps!

In such a case the fewer one's words, the less are they likely to be untrue. Fortunate is the pastor who has trained his people never to expect a funeral eulogy or any appraisal of the departed. Even more to be envied is the man who has won the reputation of never delivering an address except where the deceased has been a pillar in the church. If the minister knows how to read the Scriptures, and how to guide others up the mystic altar stairs, he will cause everyone present to feel that God is near and that he is waiting to bless.

Ideally, it should be possible to solve any such problem. That is how a man feels after he goes through many of the books on other aspects of pastoral theology. In the printed accounts of cases the physician of the soul seems almost invariably to bring about a cure, ofttimes speedily. The writer's experience does not accord with such glowing accounts. Of course they are strictly true, but they are selective, not representative. In actual life a minister often feels that he has done the will of God. Sometimes he is not certain. Occasionally he knows that if he were a surgeon he could be sued for malpractice.

Whenever a clergyman fails at a funeral there are likely to be two causes, which are closely connected: he has not depended on God for personal guidance and has not kept on working until the plans are complete. By looking back, therefore, he can see the necessity of being humble, and of depending on God in prayer.

Every case that has been before us required hours of toil, as well as all a man's God-given ability. There is no quick and easy way to comfort the people who are most concerned in a problem funeral. If the modern method of dealing with cases, one at a time, has taught us anything at all, it is that to be a good physician of souls takes a vast deal of time, as well as ability. Except during his annual vacation period, a man has to stay at home and work hard.

On the other hand, there is an untold opportunity to advance the Kingdom of God, and win friends throughout the community. Immediately after the service the results may seem to be negative, but, as we shall see erelong, the door into the hearts of the people concerned should be open wide. When others throughout the neighborhood learn that the minister is the untiring helper of everyone in distress they will think of him as the shadow of a great rock in a weary land.

The substance of the whole matter is unexpectedly simple. The man who is called of God and eager to work is sure to be guided in solving each funeral problem as it arises. If that is an ideal to which none of us has yet attained, does not the spirit of our holy faith lead the servant of the Most High to attempt the impossible?

> "Ah, but a man's reach should exceed his grasp,
> Or what's a heaven for?"

XXII. The Pastoral Opportunity

IT IS unwise to think much about pastoral problems. To the Christian minister every one of them is an opportunity. In the normal parish the problem funeral comes only occasionally. Amid all its perplexities the man of God should make ready in the spirit of accepting a privilege to serve. Such difficulties ought to call out the best that is in a minister. They should lead him to say with the apostle, "I can do all things through Christ which strengtheneth me" (Phil. 4: 13).

The pastor's opportunity starts when he comes into a new field. From the very first day, indirectly and unconsciously, by his presence and influence, he can help the new friends prepare for sorrows sure to come. Without being gloomy he can live and serve in the light of eternity. Then it will never seem strange when people in sorrow call for his ministrations as death hovers near, or if it has already come to the home.

Especially in a day when the world is at war, the pastor's main concern with believing men and women may be to comfort. At the City Temple in London, Joseph Parker used to say, "In every pew there is at least one broken heart." That is the case wherever the pews are reasonably well filled. They are more likely to be filled if the man in charge of the service brings into it at least a glimpse of the life everlasting.

In a pastoral ministry of comfort nothing is standardized. In a normal hour of worship the Christian hope may sound forth in one of the hymns or in the responsive reading. Again, there may be a New Testament lesson that breathes the assurance of peace in the presence of the last great enemy. In the pastoral prayer there should always be some word of thanksgiving for "the saints who from their labors rest," or else an entreaty for those who sit under the shadow of unexpected sorrow.

Hope is one of three notes that should dominate every hour of worship. The other two are faith and love. Just as in a painting of the Madonna by Raphael there is sure to be a glimpse of the sky, so in the public worship of God there should always be a vista of the Father's home. Especially should this be the case when the world is full of woe, and fearful of something worse to come.

TEACHING SERMONS

From time to time the regular sermon ought to deal with "the last things." As a rule this kind of preaching comes at the evening service or at vespers. If there were more teaching of Christian doctrine on Sunday evening, so that every vital truth in its turn would be as luminous now as in the Early Church, there would be less difficulty in persuading people to attend the second service. In every community there are many who wish to be sure that it is possible for the modern man to believe in the life beyond.

One way to present these Christian truths is to have a series about the Apostles' Creed. In fact, there may be two series. In the sermons that deal with the closing words of the Creed there is an opportunity to preach about "The Communion of Saints." One Sunday afternoon at the Fifth Avenue Presbyterian Church in New York City, when John S. Bonnell was speaking on the subject, everyone seemed to be hanging breathless on his words. It is good to know that while still in the flesh believers can commune with the spirits of just men and women made perfect in glory.

As for heavenly recognition, that is largely a matter of inference. About the matter no one has spoken more wisely than the aged woman in Scotland: "Mon, do ye think we'll be bigger fules in heaven than we are on earth?" Of course we shall know and love those who have been dear. We shall likewise need no introduction to the saints and martyrs of olden times. In the heavenly home there will be no formalities and no social barriers. There will be fellowship with the Father and the Son, as well as with all the children of light.

Another sermon may be about "The Resurrection of the Body." Like many a modern youth, the writer once questioned this teaching of the Scriptures. He wondered if it were possible to believe in the resurrection of the soul, but not the body. Later he discovered that there must be a death ere there can be a resurrection. Since the only part of a man that dies is the body, how could there be a resurrection of the soul?

Whether or not a man believes the doctrine, the New Testament teaches the resurrection of the body. According to the Westminster Shorter Catechism, which is in keeping with the Scriptures, "The souls of believers are at their death made perfect in holiness, and do immediately pass into glory; and their bodies, being still united to Christ, do rest in their graves, till the resurrection."

The doctrine now is the same as in days of old. But the way of presenting the truth today should be different. Doctrine is teaching. In the best schools now a good deal of the instruction is by the use of cases. Why should we not employ this method in teaching what the New Testament makes known concerning the state of the soul after death? The dying thief affords an object lesson. If his soul went at once to God, the same must be true of everyone who believes in Christ (Luke 23: 43).

Again, the text may be from Paul's classic words about the life to come. Through him we learn that the heavenly body will be spiritual, not physical (I Cor. 15: 44-49). What the nature of the spiritual body will be no one can tell. Surely there will be no such limitations as beset the present earthly tenement, in which for a few score years the soul of man finds a local habitation. For the eternal dwelling place of every redeemed soul the Lord God will provide a spiritual body like that of Christ Jesus after he arose from the grave.

Here again the teaching is partly by inference. If reverent and humble, surmise is far from wrong. When the late William G. Moorehead was seventy-seven years of age he shared with a group of us his conception of the resurrection body. For years that eloquent preacher and lecturer had been frail. Every once in a while he had been forced to undergo an operation for the removal of glands from his neck. Whimsically he told us: "Whenever I read in the Apocalypse, 'There shall be no more pain,' I paraphrase the words to read, 'There shall be no glands.'"

These popular teaching sermons ought to include one about "The Final Return of Our Lord." Here again we move in the realm of mystery. Much about the Second Coming we on earth cannot know. But, in fairness to the facts as they shine out from many a page of the New Testament, the Christian interpreter should proclaim the central truth. In some way that we do not understand, and at a time that we cannot foretell, our Lord is coming in glory, to complete the work for which he died upon the cross. "Wherefore comfort one another with these words" (I Thess. 4: 18).

In the pulpit and elsewhere the minister should make clear the Christian attitude toward death. For the child of God this experience is a sort of sleep. Beyond the sleep is the awakening in the Father's home. All these terms about death are figurative. The only way that we can speak about heaven is in the language of earth. But beneath every such figure should be a solid fact. It is that the Father God promises to take care of every redeemed child, both in death and the life that follows.

PASTORAL CARE

The same spirit of loving concern for God's children enables the pastor to care for the household when sorrow comes. After the funeral services are over, his ministry of love has only begun. On the same evening, if the way is clear, he may call at the home and lead at family prayers. In a week or ten days he may call again and see if he can help in the new adjustments. If the friends ask his advice about matters of business, he need not become involved, but he should suggest a wise counselor. In short, the pastor should be a personal friend of the family.

In the case of those whose church membership has lapsed there is an opportunity for the renewal of their old-time vows. In the home of the boy who was electrocuted accidentally, the father and mother had long been nominal Christians. But after he was with them no more, they united with the local church. They were always in their pew ahead of time on the Lord's Day, and especially at the Communion. Little by little their lives became transformed. In short, bruised hearts call for pastoral care.

After another kind of funeral there may be an opportunity to win a person or a household where religion has been practically unknown. If a man has been making money his god, or if a woman has been living for pleasure, the death of an only child may reveal the soul's need of God. In every congregation some of the saintliest persons have come to him through the sacrament of sorrow.

In a certain downtown church the membership has kept growing, despite the fact that the tides of population are away from that district. One day the sexton asked the minister if he had noticed how the church was securing the majority of the new members. The pastor thought that he knew but still he asked the sexton for an opinion. The reply was unexpected:

"Whenever people enter the church for a funeral they are likely to come back for church membership." Is it any wonder that the congregation is growing in spiritual power? Under God, one reason is that the minister knows how to conduct a funeral service, and how to follow it up by winning the new friends for Christ and the parish church. In short, he is a good shepherd.

The presence of death opens to the pastor many a door that might otherwise remain closed. If at all times he cares tenderly for the flock, and especially when there is sorrow, he should have comparatively few problem funerals among his own people. But when others out in the community learn that he has a shepherd's heart, they will turn to him in the hour of need. Gradually he should win more than a few of them for the fellowship of Christ and the church. Who save the parish minister has so many golden opportunities?

Is it any wonder that many of us look on the work of the local pastor as the most vital and the most difficult in the modern world? Nowhere else does the man of God meet such a test of his ability and training as in many a funeral. But let him not falter; the grace of God is far more than sufficient for all the needs of his ministering servant.

"The elders which are among you I exhort, who am also an elder, and a witness of the sufferings of Christ, and also a partaker of the glory that shall be revealed:

"Feed the flock of God which is among you, taking the oversight thereof, not by constraint, but willingly; not for filthy lucre, but of a ready mind;

"Neither as being lords over God's heritage, but being ensamples to the flock.

"And when the chief Shepherd shall appear, ye shall receive a crown of glory that fadeth not away" (I Peter 5: 1-4).

Inspirational Readings

Green, Peter, *The Man of God*. Hodder & Stoughton, Ltd., London, 1935.

APPENDIX

Appendix

A FUNERAL ANTHOLOGY

THE following pages show some of the funeral poems that one is able to assemble in spare hours during a few months. When the writer left the pastorate he foolishly discarded such materials. Now he welcomes the opportunity to start another anthology.

The order of the poems is somewhat mechanical. It depends in part on the number of lines that can appear on a page. There is little endeavor to put in one section the verses that deal with a given subject. Each poem bears a serial number, to aid in using the topical index.

However, the order is somewhat progressive. By watching each poem that appears at the top of a page, and ignoring the shorter verses that appear elsewhere, it is possible to trace an increasing purpose. Even so, the arrangement is dictated by personal feeling, not cold logic. The same is true of more worthy collections, such as the first series of *The Golden Treasury*, by Francis T. Palgrave.

The ensuing anthology should encourage the reader to start one of his own. The majority of these poems are worthy to appear in any garden of spiritual verse. However, a few are here for personal reasons. Many others of recent vintage would be included if the costs for such use were not prohibitive. Fortunately, there is no barrier to their being in any private anthology.

The present collection affords variety enough to suit different tastes. In any case the poem for use at a funeral should be so clear and luminous that it will impart light and beauty, if not a touch of splendor.

1.   THE BUTTERFLY

I hold you at last in my hand,
    Exquisite child of the air.
Can I ever understand
    How you grew to be so fair?

            .   .   .   .   .

Now I hold you fast in my hand,
    You marvelous butterfly,
Till you help me to understand
    The eternal mystery.

From that creeping thing in the dust
    To this shining bliss in the blue!
God give me courage to trust
    I can break my chrysalis too!
                            —*Alice Freeman Palmer*
[I John 3: 2a]

2.   DEATH IS A DOOR

Death is only an old door
Set in a garden wall;
On gentle hinges it gives, at dusk
When the thrushes call.

            .   .   .   .   .

There is nothing to trouble any heart;
Nothing to hurt at all.
Death is only a quiet door
In an old wall.
                            —*Nancy Byrd Turner*
[John 19: 41a]

3.   SEEDS

We drop a seed into the ground,
A tiny, shapeless thing, shrivelled and dry,
And, in the fulness of its time, is seen
A form of peerless beauty, robed and crowned
Beyond the pride of any earthly queen,
Instinct with loveliness, and sweet and rare,
The perfect emblem of its Maker's care.

This from a shrivelled seed?—
—Then may man hope indeed!

For man is but the seed of what he shall be,
When, in the fulness of his perfecting,
He drops the husk and cleaves his upward way,
Through earth's retardings and clinging clay,
Into the sunshine of God's perfect day.
No fetters then! No bonds of time or space!
But powers as ample as the boundless grace
That suffered man, and death, and yet in tenderness,
Set wide the door, and passed Himself before—
As He had promised—to prepare a place.

          .   .   .   .   .

We know not what we shall be—only this—
That we shall be made like Him—as He is.
                                    —*John Oxenham*

[John 12: 24]

4.   WHERE TO FIND GOD

As the marsh-hen secretly builds on the watery sod,
Behold I will build me a nest on the greatness of God:
I will fly in the greatness of God as the marsh-hen flies
In the freedom that fills all the space 'twixt the marsh and the skies:
By so many roots as the marsh-grass sends in the sod
I will heartily lay me a-hold on the greatness of God:
Oh, like to the greatness of God is the greatness within
The range of the marshes, the liberal marshes of Glynn.
                                              —*Sidney Lanier*

[Isa. 40: 28]

5.

" 'Tis the weakness in strength, that I cry for! my flesh, that I seek
In the Godhead! I seek and I find it. O Saul, it shall be
A face like my face that receives thee; a Man like to me,
Thou shalt love and be loved by, forever: a Hand like this hand
Shall throw open the gates of new life to thee! See the Christ stand!"
                                              —*Robert Browning*

[Heb. 4: 15]

6.

So, through the thunder comes a human voice
Saying, "O heart I made, a heart beats here!
Face, my hands fashioned, see it in myself!
Thou hast no power nor mayst conceive of mine,
But love I gave thee, with myself to love,
And thou must love me who have died for thee!"
                                              —*Robert Browning*

[I Peter 2: 21]

7.   BEYOND THE HORIZON

When men go down to the sea in ships,
'Tis not to the sea they go;
Some isle or pole the mariners' goal,
And thither they sail through calm and gale,
When down to the sea they go.

When souls go down to the sea by ship,
And the dark ship's name is Death,
Why mourn and wail at the vanishing sail?
Though outward bound, God's world is round,
And only a ship is Death.

When I go down to the sea by ship,
And Death unfurls her sail,
Weep not for me, for there will be
A living host on another coast
To beckon and cry, "All hail!"

—*Robert Freeman*

[Ps. 107: 23]

8.   THE ETERNAL VOYAGE

Is this the end? I know it cannot be.
Our ships shall sail upon another sea;
New islands yet shall break upon our sight,
New continents of love and truth and might.

—*John White Chadwick*

[II Tim. 4: 6-8]

9.   IN ANOTHER ROOM

No, not cold beneath the grasses,
  Not close-walled within the tomb;
Rather, in our Father's mansion,
  Living, in another room.

Living, like the man who loves me,
  Like my child with cheeks abloom,
Out of sight, at desk or schoolbook,
  Busy, in another room.

Nearer than my son whom fortune
  Beckons where the strange lands loom;
Just behind the hanging curtain,
  Serving, in another room.

Shall I doubt my Father's mercy?
  Shall I think of death as doom,
Or the stepping o'er the threshold
  To a bigger, brighter room?

Shall I blame my Father's wisdom?
  Shall I sit enswathed in gloom,
When I know my loves are happy,
  Waiting in another room?

                              —*Robert Freeman*

[John 14: 2]

10.   NIGHTFALL

Fold up the tent!
The sun is in the West.
To-morrow my untented soul will range
Among the blest.
    And I am well content,
    For what is sent, is sent,
    And God knows best.

Fold up the tent,
And speed the parting guest!
The night draws on, though night and day are one
On this long quest.
    This house was only lent
    For my apprenticement—
    What is, is best.

Fold up the tent!
Its tenant would be gone,
To fairer skies than mortal eyes
May look upon.
    All that I loved has passed,
    And left me at the last
    Alone!—alone!

Fold up the tent!
Above the mountain's crest,
I hear a clear voice calling, calling clear,—
"To rest! To rest!"
    And I am glad to go,
    For the sweet oil is low,
    And rest is best!

                                 —*John Oxenham*

[II Cor. 5: 1]

11. REST FOR THE WEARY

The camel at the close of day
    Kneels down upon the sandy plain
To have his burden lifted off
    And rest again.

My soul, thou too shouldst to thy knees
    When daylight draweth to a close,
And let thy Master lift thy load,
    And grant repose.

Else how canst thou tomorrow meet,
    With all tomorrow's work to do,
If thou thy burden all the night
    Dost carry through?

The camel kneels at break of day
    To have his guide replace his load,
Then rises up anew to take
    The desert road.

So thou shouldst kneel at morning dawn
    That God may give thee daily care,
Assured that He no load too great
    Will make thee bear.
                              —*Anna Temple Whitney*
[Matt. 11: 28-30]

12.   "NONE OTHER LAMB"

None other Lamb, none other Name,
    None other Hope in heaven or earth or sea,
None other Hiding-place from guilt and shame,
    None beside Thee.

My faith burns low, my hope burns low
    Only my heart's desire cries out in me
By the deep thunder of its want and woe
    Cries out to Thee.

Lord, Thou art Life tho' I be dead,
    Love's Fire Thou art, however cold I be:
Nor heaven have I, nor place to lay my head,
    Nor home, but Thee.
                                        —*Christina G. Rossetti*
[Rev. 21: 23]

13.   "BABY SLEEPS"

            The baby wept;
The mother took it from the nurse's arms,
And hushed its fears, and soothed its vain alarms,
            And baby slept.

            Again it weeps,
And God doth take it from the mother's arms,
From present griefs, and future unknown harms,
            And baby sleeps.
                                        —*Samuel Hinds*
[Isa. 66: 13]

14.   THE SLEEP

Of all the thoughts of God that are
Borne inward into souls afar,
Along the Psalmist's music deep,
Now tell me if any is,
For gift or grace, surpassing this:
"He giveth his belovèd—sleep"?

    .   .   .   .

"Sleep soft," beloved! we sometimes say,
Who have no tune to charm away
Sad dreams that through the eyelids creep:
But never doleful dream again
Shall break the happy slumber when
He giveth *his* belovèd—sleep.

    .   .   .   .

Ay, men may wonder while they scan
A living, thinking, feeling man
Confirmed in such a rest to keep;
But Angels say, and through the word
I think their happy smile is *heard*—
"He giveth his belovèd—sleep."

    .   .   .   .

And friends, dear friends, when it shall be
That this low breath is gone from me,
And round my bier ye come to weep,
Let One, most loving of you all,
Say, "Not a tear must o'er her fall!
He giveth his belovèd sleep."
                              —*Elizabeth Barrett Browning*

[Ps. 127: 2]

15.   THE ANGEL OF PATIENCE

To weary hearts, to mourning homes,
God's meekest Angel gently comes:
No power has he to banish pain,
Or give us back our lost again;
And yet in tenderest love, our dear
And Heavenly Father sends him here.

There's quiet in the Angel's glance,
There's rest in his still countenance!
He mocks no grief with idle cheer,
Nor wounds with words the mourner's ear;
But ills and woes he may not cure
He kindly trains us to endure.

                    —*John Greenleaf Whittier*
[Heb. 1: 14]

16.   TO A WATERFOWL

    He who, from zone to zone,
Guides through the boundless sky thy certain flight,
In the long way that I must tread alone,
    Will lead my steps aright.

                    —*William Cullen Bryant*
[Ps. 139: 9, 10]

17.   CLEANSING FIRES

Let thy gold be cast in the furnace,
    The red gold, precious and bright;
Do not fear the hungry fire,
    With its caverns of burning light;
And thy gold shall return more precious,
    Free from every spot and stain;
For gold must be tried by fire,
    As a heart must be tried by pain!

In the cruel fire of Sorrow
    Cast thy heart, do not faint or wail;
Let thy hand be firm and steady
    Do not let thy spirit quail:
But wait till the trial is over
    And take thy heart again;
For as gold is tried by fire,
    So a heart must be tried by pain!

I shall know by the gleam and the glitter
    Of the golden chain you wear,
By your heart's calm strength in loving,
    Of the fire they have had to bear.
Beat on, true heart, forever!
    Shine bright, strong golden chain!
And bless the cleansing fire,
    And the furnace of living pain!
                                    —*Adelaide Anne Proctor*
[Job 23: 10]

18.   THE STRUGGLE

Say not the struggle nought availeth,
    The labor and the wounds are vain,
The enemy faints not, nor faileth,
    And as things have been they remain.

If hopes were dupes, fears may be liars;
    It may be, in yon smoke concealed,
Your comrades chase e'en now the fliers,
    And, but for you, possess the field.

For while the tired waves, vainly breaking,
    Seem here no painful inch to gain,
Far back, through creeks and inlets making,
    Comes silent, flooding in, the main.

And not by eastern windows only,
    When daylight comes, comes in the light,
In front, the sun climbs slow, how slowly;
    But westward, look, the land is bright.

—*Arthur Hugh Clough*

[Ps. 130: 6]

19.   THE ASSURANCE

Because in tender love He stooped for me,
And suffered on the Cross in agony,
I longed for Him to come and set me free,—
    Because He died for me.

—*Betty Scott Stam*

[I Thess. 5: 10]

20.   RABBI BEN EZRA

Grow old along with me!
The best is yet to be,
The last of life, for which the first was made:
Our times are in his hand
Who saith, "A whole I planned,
Youth shows but half; trust God: see all, nor be afraid!"

    .   .   .   .   .

All that is, at all,
Lasts ever, past recall;
Earth changes, but thy soul and God stand sure:
What entered into thee,
That was, is, and shall be:
Time's wheel runs back or stops: Potter and clay endure.

    .   .   .   .   .

So, take and use thy work:
Amend what flaws may lurk,
What strain o' the stuff, what warpings past the aim!
My times be in thy hand!
Perfect the cup as planned!
Let age approve of youth, and death complete the same!
                                        —*Robert Browning*

[Ps. 91: 14-16]

21.

Speak to Him, thou, for He hears, and Spirit with Spirit can meet—
Closer is He than breathing, and nearer than hands and feet.
                                        —*Alfred Tennyson*

[Heb. 4: 15, 16]

22. THE ETERNAL GOODNESS

I see the wrong that round me lies,
  I feel the guilt within;
I hear, with groan and travail-cries,
  The world confess its sin.

Yet, in the maddening maze of things,
  And tossed by storm and flood,
To one fixed trust my spirit clings;
  I know that God is good!

    .   .   .   .   .

I long for household voices gone,
  For vanished smiles I long,
But God hath led my dear ones on,
  And He can do no wrong.

I know not what the future hath
  Of marvel or surprise,
Assured alone that life and death
  His mercy underlies.

    .   .   .   .   .

And so beside the Silent Sea
  I wait the muffled oar;
No harm from Him can come to me
  On ocean or on shore.

I know not where His islands lift
  Their fronded palms in air;
I only know I cannot drift
  Beyond His love and care.
                    —*John Greenleaf Whittier*
[Rev. 22: 2]

23.   RESIGNATION

There is no flock, however watched and tended,
 But one dead lamb is there!
There is no fireside, howsoe'er defended,
 But has one vacant chair!

The air is full of farewells to the dying,
 And mournings for the dead;
The heart of Rachel, for her children crying,
 Will not be comforted!

Let us be patient! These severe afflictions
 Not from the ground arise,
But oftentimes celestial benedictions
 Assume this dark disguise.

We see but dimly through the mists and vapors;
 Amid these earthly damps
What seem to us but sad, funereal tapers
 May be heaven's distant lamps.

There is no Death! What seems so is transition;
 This life of mortal breath
Is but a suburb of the life elysian,
 Whose portal we call Death.
      —*Henry Wadsworth Longfellow*

[Rom. 8: 28]

24.   A MOTHER'S FAREWELL

Dear Lord, receive my son, whose winning love
To me was like a friendship, far above
The course of nature or his tender age,
Whose looks could all my bitter griefs assuage;
Let his pure soul ordained sev'n years to be
In that frail body, which was part of me,
Remain my pledge in Heav'n, as sent to show
How to this port with ev'ry step I go.

—John Beaumont

[Luke 2: 40]

25.   A FATHER'S LOVE

I walked with one whose child had lately died.
We passed the little folk in the street at play,
When suddenly a clear voice "Father!" cried.
The man turned quick and glad; sighed; moved away.

I spoke not, but 'twas given me to discern
The love that watches through eternal years.
God surely must so start and quickly turn
Whene'er the cry of "Father!" strikes His ears.

—William Canton

[Ps. 103: 13]

26.

He lives, he wakes,—'tis Death is dead, not he.

—Percy Bysshe Shelley

[John 3: 36a]

27.   THE OPEN DOOR

You, my son,
Have shown me God,
Your kiss upon my cheek
Has made me feel the gentle touch
Of him who leads us on.
The memory of your smile, when young,
Reveals his face,
As mellowing years come on apace.
And when you went before,
You left the gates of heaven ajar
That I might glimpse,
Approaching from afar,
The glories of his grace.
Hold, son, my hand,
Guide me along the path,
That, coming,
I may stumble not
Nor roam,
Nor fail to show the way
Which leads us—home.

> —*Grace Coolidge, written in memory
> of Calvin Coolidge, Jr., on the fifth
> anniversary of his death*

[Luke 2: 52]

28.

"A soul released from prison
Is risen, is risen,—
Is risen to the glory of the Lord."

> —*John Oxenham*

[II Tim. 4: 6]

29. A SONG OF THANKSGIVING

Saints are God's flowers, fragrant souls
  That His own hand hath planted,
Not in some far-off heavenly place,
  Or solitude enchanted,
But here and there and everywhere,—
  In lonely field, or crowded town,
  God sees a flower when He looks down.

     .   .   .   .   .

One such I knew,—and had the grace
  To thank my God for knowing:
The beauty of her quiet life
  Was like a rose in blowing,
So fair and sweet, so all-complete
  And all unconscious, as a flower,
  That light and fragrance were her dower.

     .   .   .   .   .

A vow to keep her life alive
  In deeds of pure affection,
So that her love shall find in them
  A daily resurrection;
A constant prayer that they may wear
  Some touch of that supernal light
  With which she blossoms in God's sight.

                        —*Henry van Dyke*

[Prov. 31: 29-31]

30. FAREWELL IN AUTUMN

Not in winter, not in storm,
Nor when spring's buds are calling,
But in autumn's quiet charm,
While russet leaves are falling.

The good earth turns herself to rest,
After her time of growing,
Drawing her children to her breast,
To wait a richer sowing.

So in his autumn's golden day,
His earthly life forsaking,
In quiet peace he passed away,
To meet the last awaking.
                                    —*Will C. Osborn*

[Job 5: 26]

31. GOD'S HANDWRITING

He writes in characters too grand
For our short sight to understand;
We catch but broken strokes, and try
To fathom all the mystery
Of withered hopes, of death, of life,
The endless war, the useless strife,—
But there, with larger, clearer sight,
We shall see this—His way was right.
                                    —*John Oxenham*

[I Cor. 13: 12]

32. A MISSIONARY MARTYR

(A favorite poem of Betty Scott Stam)

Afraid? Of what?
To feel the spirit's glad release?
To pass from pain to perfect peace?
The strife and strain of life to cease?
Afraid—of that?

Afraid? Of what?
Afraid to see the Saviour's face?
To hear His welcome, and to trace
The glory gleam from wounds of grace?
Afraid—of that?

Afraid? Of what?
A flash—a crash—a piercèd heart!
Darkness—light—O heaven's art!
Each wound of His a counterpart!
Afraid—of that?

Afraid? Of what?
To do by death what life could not?
Baptize with blood a stony plot
Till souls shall blossom from the spot?
Afraid—of that?

—*E. H. Hamilton*

[Ps. 23: 4]

33.   THE MEANING OF DEATH

We are so stupid about death. We will not learn
How it is wages paid to those who earn,
How it is gift for which on earth we yearn,
To be set free from bondage to the flesh;
How it is turning seed-corn into grain,
How it is winning heaven's eternal gain,
How it means freedom ever more from pain.
            How it untangles every mortal mesh.

We are so selfish about death, we count our grief
Far more than we consider their relief
Whom the great Reaper gathers in the sheaf
No more to know the season's constant change:
And we forget that it means only life.
                              —*William C. Doane*

[Rev. 14: 15]

34.   THE DOOR OF DEATH

The door of Death is made of gold,
That mortal eyes cannot behold;
But when the mortal eyes are closed,
And cold and pale the limbs reposed,
The soul awakes, and, wond'ring, sees
In her mild hand the golden keys.
The grave is heaven's golden gate,
And rich and poor around it wait.
                              —*William Blake*

[Rev. 22: 14]

35.   PROSPICE

Fear death?—to feel the fog in my throat,
    The mist in my face,
When the snows begin, and the blasts denote
    I am nearing the place,
The power of the night, the press of the storm,
    The post of the foe;
Where he stands, the Arch Fear in a visible form,
    Yet the strong man must go:
For the journey is done and the summit attained,
    And the barriers fall,
Though a battle's to fight ere the guerdon be gained,
    The reward of it all.
I was ever a fighter, so—one fight more,
    The best and the last!
I would hate that death bandaged my eyes, and forbore,
    And bade me creep past.
No! let me taste the whole of it, fare like my peers
    The heroes of old,
Bear the brunt, in a minute pay glad life's arrears
    Of pain, darkness and cold.
For sudden the worst turns the best to the brave,
    The black minute's at end,
And the elements' rage, the fiend-voices that rave,
    Shall dwindle, shall blend,
Shall change, shall become first a peace out of pain,
    Then a light, then thy breast,
O thou soul of my soul! I shall clasp thee again,
    And with God be the rest!

                                    —*Robert Browning*

[Rev. 2: 10]

36.   GOING TO HEAVEN

Going to heaven!
I don't know when,
Pray do not ask me how,—
Indeed, I'm too astonished
To think of answering you!
Going to heaven!—
How dim it sounds!
And yet it will be done
As sure as flocks go home at night
Unto the shepherd's arm!
                                    —*Emily Dickinson*

[Ps. 23: 6]

37.   THE UPPER ROOMS

Father, in joy our knees we bow.
This earth is not a place of tombs.
We are but in the nursery now;
        They in the upper rooms.

For are we not at home in Thee,
And all this world a visioned show?
For, knowing what Abroad is, we
        What Home is too shall know.
                                    —*George MacDonald*

[John 14: 2]

38.

They call it death, when lo! it is my birth.
                                    —*Robert Freeman*

[John 11: 25]

39.   EMANCIPATION

Why be afraid of death
As though your life were breath?
       Death but anoints your eyes
       With clay, O glad surprise!
Why should you be forlorn?
Death only husks the corn.
       Why should you fear to meet
       The Thresher of the wheat?
Is sleep a thing to dread?
Yet, sleeping you are dead
       Till you awake and rise,
       Here, or beyond the skies.
Why should it be a wrench
To leave your wooden bench?
       Why not, with happy shout,
       Run home when school is out?
The dear ones left behind?
O foolish one and blind,
       A day, and you will meet;
       A night, and you will greet.
This is the death of death:
To breathe away a breath,
       And know the end of strife,
       And taste the deathless life,
And joy without a fear,
And smile without a tear,
       And work, nor care nor rest,
       And find the last the best.
               —*Maltbie D. Babcock*

[Heb. 2: 15]

40.

Here in the body pent,
   Absent from Him I roam,
Yet nightly pitch my moving tent
   A day's march nearer home.
               —*James Montgomery*
[II Peter 1: 13, 14]

41.   WITH US NO MORE

It singeth low in every heart,
    We hear it each and all—
A song of those who answer not,
    However we may call;
They throng the silence of the breast,
    We see them as of yore—
The kind, the brave, the sweet,
    Who walk with us no more.

'Tis hard to take the burden up
    When these have laid it down;
They brightened all the joy of life,
    They softened every frown;
But, Oh, 'tis good to think of them
    When we are troubled sore!
Thanks be to God that such have been,
    Although they are no more.

More homelike seems the vast unknown
    Since they have entered there;
To follow them were not so hard,
    Wherever they may fare;
They cannot be where God is not,
    On any sea or shore;
Whate'er betides, thy love abides,
    Our God, forever more.
                        —*John White Chadwick*

[Heb. 12; 1]

42.   IN MEMORIAM

Strong Son of God, immortal Love,
  Whom we, that have not seen thy face,
  By faith, and faith alone, embrace,
Believing where we cannot prove;

.   .   .   .   .

Thou wilt not leave us in the dust:
  Thou madest man, he knows not why,
  He thinks he was not made to die;
And thou hast made him: thou art just.

Thou seemest human and divine,
  The highest, holiest manhood, thou.
  Our wills are ours, we know not how;
Our wills are ours, to make them thine.

.   .   .   .   .

We have but faith: we cannot know,
  For knowledge is of things we see;
  And yet we trust it comes from thee,
A beam in darkness: let it grow.

.   .   .   .   .

Forgive my grief for one removed,
  Thy creature, whom I found so fair.
  I trust he lives in thee, and there
I find him worthier to be loved.

Forgive these wild and wandering cries,
  Confusions of a wasted youth;
  Forgive them where they fail in truth,
And in thy wisdom make me wise.
                          —Alfred Tennyson

[John 14: 6]

43. A BETTER RESURRECTION

I have no wit, no words, no tears;
　My heart within me like a stone
Is numbed too much for hopes or fears;
　Look right, look left, I dwell alone;
I lift mine eyes, but dimmed with grief
　No everlasting hills I see;
My life is in the falling leaf:
　　O Jesus, quicken me.

My life is like a faded leaf,
　My harvest dwindled to a husk;
Truly my life is void and brief
　And tedious in the barren dusk;
My life is like a frozen thing,
　No bud nor greenness can I see:
Yet rise it shall—the sap of Spring;
　　O Jesus, rise in me.

My life is like a broken bowl,
　A broken bowl that cannot hold
One drop of water for my soul
　Or cordial in the searching cold;
Cast in the fire the perished thing,
　Melt and remould it, till it be
A royal cup for Him my King:
　　O Jesus, drink of me.

　　　　　　　　　　—Christina G. Rossetti
[Eccl. 12: 6]

44. TRIUMPH OVER DEATH

Vital spark of heavenly flame!
Quit, oh quit this mortal frame:
  Trembling, hoping, lingering, flying,
  Oh the pain, the bliss of dying!
Cease, fond Nature, cease thy strife,
And let me languish into life.

Hark! they whisper; Angels say,
Sister Spirit, come away.
  What is this absorbs me quite?
  Steals my senses, shuts my sight,
Drowns my spirit, draws my breath?
Tell me, my Soul, can this be Death?

The world recedes; it disappears!
Heaven opens on my eyes! my ears
  With sounds seraphic ring:
  Lend, lend your wings! I mount! I fly!
O Grave! where is thy victory?
  O Death! where is thy sting?
             —*Alexander Pope*

[I Cor. 15: 55]

45.

I will not faint, but trust in God
  Who this my lot hath given:
He leads me by the thorny road
  Which is the road to heaven.
Though sad my day that lasts so long,
At evening I shall have a song:
Though dim my day until the night,
At evening-time there shall be light.
            —*Christina G. Rossetti*

[Zech. 14: 7]

46.   RESURGENCE

Though he that, ever kind and true,
Kept stoutly step by step with you,
Your whole long, gusty lifetime through,
    Be gone a while before—
Be now a moment gone before—
Yet doubt not; soon the season shall restore
    Your friend to you.

He has but turned the corner—still
He pushes on with right good will
Through mire and marsh, by dale and hill
    The selfsame arduous way—
That selfsame, upland, hopeful way,
That you and he, through many a doubtful day
    Attempted still.

He is not dead—this friend—not dead,
But in the path we mortals tread
Got some few trifling steps ahead,
    And nearer to the end;
So that you, too, once past the bend,
Shall meet again, as face to face, this friend
    You fancy dead.

Push gaily on, brave heart, the while
You travel forward mile by mile,
He loiters, with a backward smile,
    Till you can overtake;
And strains his eyes to search his wake,
Or, whistling as he sees you through the brake,
    Waits on a stile.

                              —*Robert Louis Stevenson*

[Heb. 11: 4c]

47. GOD OF THE LIVING

God of the living, in whose eyes
Unveiled the whole creation lies!
All souls are thine; we must not say
That those are dead who pass away;
From this our world of flesh set free;
We know them living unto thee.

Released from earthly toil and strife,
With thee is hidden still their life;
Thine are their thoughts, their words, their powers,
All thine, and yet most truly ours:
For well we know, where'er they be,
Our dead are living unto thee.

Not spilt like water on the ground,
Not wrapt in dreamless sleep profound,
Not wandering in unknown despair
Beyond thy voice, thine arm, thy care;
Not left to lie like fallen tree;
Not dead, but living unto thee.

O Breather into man of breath!
O Holder of the keys of death!
O Giver of the life within!
Save us from death, the death of sin;
That body, soul, and spirit be
Forever living unto thee!
                              —*John Ellerton*

[II Sam. 14: 14b]

48.   THE RIVER OF LIFE

We know not a voice of that River,
   If vocal or silent it be,
Where for ever and ever and ever
    It flows to no sea.

.   .   .   .   .

Oh goodly the banks of that River,
   Oh goodly the fruits that they bear,
Where for ever and ever and ever
    It flows and is fair.

For lo on each bank of that River
   The Tree of Life life-giving grows,
Where for ever and ever and ever
    The Pure River flows.
                 —*Christina G. Rossetti*

[Rev. 22: 2]

49.   ALL'S WELL!

Is the burden past your bearing?
   God's in His heaven!
Hopeless?—Friendless?—No one caring?
   God's in His heaven!
Burdens shared are light to carry,
Love shall come though long He tarry.
   All's well! All's well!
                 —*John Oxenham*

[Ps. 55: 22]

50.   A RAINBOW O'ER A GRAVE

The record of a faith sublime,
   And hope, through clouds far-off discerned;
   The incense of a love that burned
Through pain and doubt defying Time:

The story of a soul at strife
   That learned at last to kiss the rod,
   And passed through sorrow up to God,
From living to a higher life:

A light that gleams across the wave
   Of darkness, down the rolling years,
   Piercing the heavy mist of tears—
A rainbow shining o'er a grave.
                —Henry van Dyke

[Heb. 11:5]

51.   A RAINBOW O'ER THE CROSS

O Joy that seekest me through pain,
   I cannot close my heart to thee;
I trace the rainbow through the rain,
And feel the promise is not vain
   That morn shall tearless be.
              —George Matheson

[Gen. 9: 13]

52.   AT THE BURIAL

Lord of all Light and Darkness,
   Lord of all Life and Death,
Behold, we lay in earth today
   The flesh that perisheth.

Take to Thyself whatever may
   Be not as dust and breath,—
Lord of all Light and Darkness,
   Lord of all Life and Death.
                —*William Watson*
[Ps. 103: 14]

53. THE REDEEMED IN GLORY

From North and South, and East and West,
      They come!
The sorely tried, the much oppressed,
Their Faith and Love to manifest,
      They come!
They come to tell of work well done,
They come to tell of kingdoms won,
To worship at the Great White Throne,
      They come!
In a noble consecration,
With a sound of jubilation,
    They come! They come!
               —*John Oxenham*
[Rev. 5: 9, 10]

54. No little child has ever come from God and stayed a brief while, returning again to the Father, without making glad the home, and leaving behind some trace of heaven. The family would count themselves poorer without those quaint sayings, those cunning caresses, that soft touch, that sudden smile. This short visit was not an incident; it was a benediction.—*John Watson.*
[Matt. 19: 14]

55. This life is but the cradle of the other. Of what importance, then, are illness and time, old age and death? They are but stages in the transformation that has its beginnings here below. . . . The evening of life bears its own lamp.—*Joseph Joubert.*
[Rom. 8: 38, 39]

56. I have lived. I have labored. I have loved. To love and labor is the sum of living. Now the day is far spent, and the night is at hand. The time draweth nigh when man shall rest from his labors. But still he shall love, and he shall enter into rest through Him who is Light, and Life, and Love.—*Sir Thomas More.*
[Luke 24: 29]

57. We do not believe in immortality because we have proved it, but, we forever try to prove it because we believe it.—*James Martineau.*
[Acts 26: 8]

58. First learn to love one living man;
     Then mayst thou think upon the dead.
     [I John 3: 14a]

Index of Scripture Passages

Index of Subjects

Accident, Death by, 14, 138, 172, 174, 191

Aged Person, 80, 88, 100, 147, 193, 206, Poems 20, 50

Anniversary Date, 171, 172

Anthems, List of, 95, 96

Anthology, Funeral, 211-245

Apostles' Creed, 41, 153

Army, U. S., 162-169, 181

Arrangements, Practical, 57-63: preliminary, 57-62; final, 62, 63

"Assisting" Minister, 60-62, 185

Attire, Pastor's, 15, 71

Beauty, 67, 73, 90, 92, 93, 98, 100, 112, 130, 139, 150, Poem 1

Benediction, 68, 106, 109, 110, 124, 153

Books About Funerals, 24, 36, 56, 63, 78, 96, 105, 124, 133, 167, 176, 182, 187, 207

Books of Forms, 78, 79, 85, 97

Boy, Growing, 138, 147, 191

Bulletin, Church, 171

Businessman, 22, 149

Cases, Actual: a friend with faith, 13; an awkward squad, 14; two young pastors, 15; a businessman, 22; a veteran clergyman, 24; a pastoral letter, 28; an emergency, 33; a self-trained pastor, 35; a deathbed conversion, 38; an untrained pastor, 42, 43; two lingering illnesses, 45; a pastoral inquisition, 46; a deathbed confession, 47, 48; silence, golden, 49; a home funeral, 68; a church funeral, 72-74, 84; a minister's blunder, 100; two schoolmasters, 126-128; a laymen on funeral sermons, 134; a sensationalist, 136; a pastoral com-

forter, 137; a growing boy, 137, 138; an old-fashioned sermon, 145; at the grave, 151; draping the grave, 154; a sad anniversary, 172; a disinterment, 175; a shyster undertaker, 178; an overcharge, 181; a pastor's dilemma, 185; a suicide, 188-191; a street fatality, 191-193; a profligate, 193-194; a prostitute, 194, 195; a young criminal, 195, 196; a question unanswered, 196; a clergyman's failure, 197; evangelism, 199; a sermon on communion of saints, 203; the ideal pastor, 207

Check List, Pastor's, 59, 60

Child, 55, 91, 120, 146, 147, 245

Christian Science, 20

Church, Services at the, 69-74, 93

Churches: The Church of England in Ireland, 155; The Church of Scotland, 118, 122, 155; The Methodist Church, 53, 120; The Presbyterian Church of England, 55, 116, 117, 121, 123; The Protestant Episcopal Church, 55, 116; The Roman Catholic Church, 54; The United Free Church of Scotland, 116

Climactic Stages in a Service, 81, 82

Code, Funeral, 183-187

Confession, Deathbed, 47-50, 184; assurance of pardon, 49, 50

Costs, Rising, 18, 19, 86, 177-182, 184, 190

Cremation, 156-158, 174-176

Deacons, Financial Aid by, 18, 184

Deathbed, 20, 37-56, 173, 184

Duets and Solos, List of, 96

Emergency, 33, 40, 183, 189

251